Advance Pra
HOMOSEXUALITY and the BIBLE

"Homosexuality and the Bible is a timely contribution that should be read by all sides in the debate that threatens to divide all churches. I know of no other work that so clearly illumines the biblical issues at the heart of the controversy surrounding homosexuality."

—STANLEY HAUERWAS
Gilbert T. Rowe Professor of Theological Ethics, Duke Divinity School

"This is an excellent contribution to a debate which is set to run and run in most parts of Christendom. I know of no finer presentation of all the main issues. The authors set out their cases and responses to one another with rigour and yet with an admirable absence of rancour. Be warned: this book may force you to change your mind!"

—GRAHAM STANTON
Lady Margaret's Professor of Divinity, University of Cambridge

"The issue of homosexuality before the church is indeed a wearisome task, and people of good will on both sides of the vexing question wish we could for a while talk about something else. But of course that is not possible because not only are there *real issues* at stake, but the lives of *real people* are at risk around the issue. This book presents the key arguments, pro and con, with clarity, reasoned thought, and for the most part with civil discourse. We will wait, along with Via and Gagnon, to be led to newness beyond competing advocacies to a new chapter yet to be written. That of course is the work of the Spirit. . . ."

—WALTER BRUEGGEMANN
William Marcellus McPheeters Professor Emeritus of Old Testament
Columbia Theological Seminary

"With unmatched clarity, the two sides of the homosex debate are set forth. Persons who read this volume will make their decision 'knowing the issues.'"

—CHARLES H. TALBERT
Distinguished Professor of Religion, Baylor University

"This particular dialogue book should further the discussion of this important matter, as it lays out well the exegetical, hermeneutical, and personal issues involved and at stake. Highly recommended."

—BEN WITHERINGTON III
Professor of New Testament, Asbury Theological Seminary

"Two esteemed New Testament scholars claim the Bible as ultimate authority for Christian faith and life, address the biblical witness regarding homosexuality, and come to strikingly different conclusions. How can this be? Issues of exegetical meaning and theological method are pivotal, and the interpretive choices confronting us are here clearly on display. Christian leaders and churches challenged by questions surrounding the voice and role of Scripture on same-sex relations will find in this dialogue an invaluable chart for navigating these confusing waters.

—JOEL B. GREEN
Dean of the School of Theology and Professor of New Testament
Interpretation, Asbury Theological Seminary

"Here, in brief and eminently readable form, are presented two opposing views of the controversy that rages within our churches. Robert Gagnon's brilliant and lucid condensation of his principle arguments should be a significant asset for clergy and laity alike, while Dan Via opens new vistas and challenges."

—CATHERINE CLARK KROEGER
Associate Professor of Classical and Ministry Studies,
Gordon Conwell Theological Seminary

"This book presents a vigorous and illuminating debate about the implications of scripture for contemporary attitudes toward homosexuality. While I find Via's arguments more cogent, the debate itself will be quite helpful to Christians as they think through their own positions in light of scripture. I strongly recommend this book."

—JAMES F. CHILDRESS
Hollingsworth Professor of Ethics,
University of Virginia

"Two adept spokespersons propound contrasting ways of listening to Scripture on the question of same-sex erotic relationships. Readers who already hold positions on either extreme will likely find here only reinforcement for their views. But the great, often silent, majority in the middle that struggles with this vexing issue will find provocative material on both sides that begs for critical reflection."

—ROBERT L. BRAWLEY
Albert G. McGaw Professor of New Testament,
McCormick Theological Seminary

HOMOSEXUALITY and the BIBLE

TWO VIEWS

DAN O. VIA
and
ROBERT A. J. GAGNON

FORTRESS PRESS
Minneapolis

HOMOSEXUALITY AND THE BIBLE
Two Views

Cover design: Brad Norr

ISBN 0-8006-3618-X

Manufactured in the U.S.A.
07   06   05   04   3   4   5   6   7   8   9   10

Contents

Preface   *vii*

The Bible, the Church, and Homosexuality
DAN O. VIA

Introduction   1
The Authority of the Bible   2
Hermeneutics: The Problem of Interpretation   2
Changing Attitudes   3
The Old Testament   4
Transition to the New Testament   9
The New Testament   11
Homosexual Orientation   15
Defense of the Traditional Position   18
Wandering in the Wilderness   28
A Way Forward   29

The Bible and Homosexual Practice: Key Issues

ROBERT A. J. GAGNON

On Determining What Matters in Scripture 41
The Proper Use of Analogies 43
Love and Grace from the Perspective of Jesus and Paul 50
The Pervasive Stance against Homosexual Practice
   in the Old Testament 56
The Levitical Proscriptions and the Issue of Purity 62
The Witness of Jesus 68
The Witness of Paul 74
Concluding Thoughts 88

Response to Robert A. J. Gagnon

DAN O. VIA

93

Response to Dan O. Via

ROBERT A. J. GAGNON

99

Select Bibliography 106
Index of Scripture 112

Preface

WHAT STANCE SHOULD Christians and Christian churches take regarding homosexuality? How are gay and lesbian Christians to participate in the ongoing life of the Christian community? Open dialogue in the church on these topics is still fairly recent and difficult. Sexual identity is so fundamental to our personal identity that these questions are not simple decisions but cut to the core of our humanity. The issues at stake are complex and include biblical interpretation, biology, psychology, sociology, law, ethics, and church politics. Furthermore, there are deep emotions manifested in the church's discussions: guilt, shame, anger, fear, and embarrassment about discussing in public issues surrounding such deeply private matters. A key point of contention is the biblical witness—its meaning, use, and authority.

In this brief book, two New Testament scholars examine the biblical passages on the subject of same-sex sexual behavior and how this relates to modern questions of construing homosexuality and sexual orientation. Discussing both Old Testament and New Testament passages, each author also raises important interpretive and moral questions and then offers a response to the other's assumptions, assertions, and conclusions.

Chief questions examined by professors Via and Gagnon include the distinctions between purity systems and sin, the church's use of ancient Israel's laws, the nature of the practices Paul was addressing, how the biblical passages relate to our contemporary concerns, the church's treatment of members who are homosexuals, and the assumptions we bring to reading the Bible in our modern contexts. Neither author addresses questions relating to bisexuals, transgendered persons, or intersexed persons (hermaphrodites)—all of which would have necessitated a longer volume.

It is hoped that these contributions will inform readers, enliven the discussion, and bring fresh perspective to these issues—for personal reflection, in congregational study groups, in college and seminary courses, and in church judicatory assemblies. If the result is more grace, more justice, and more community, then the church will be well served.

Dan O. Via's Acknowledgments

This presentation is based on two talks that I gave in November 2001 to the adult education forum of Saint Paul's Memorial Church (Episcopal) in Charlottesville, Virginia, where my wife and I are parishioners. I should like to dedicate it to my fellow-seekers who make this forum such a rewarding teaching context.

I am very grateful to several friends and colleagues who have given this piece helpful critical readings: Julian Hartt, Stanley Hauerwas, Nathan Scott, George Telford, and Walter Wink. I also want to thank my wife, Margaret, for the tremendous help she has given me in preparing this manuscript.

Robert A. J. Gagnon's Acknowledgments

Since the publication of my book *The Bible and Homosexual Practice: Texts and Hermeneutics* (Abingdon, 2001), some colleges and many groups in mainline denominations have invited me to give presentations on this issue. These presentations have helped me to summarize a 500-page book and to hone further a number of points. In addition, I have written several articles on this issue since the publication of my book and, in the course of writing this essay, developed more new material. This essay, then, should be viewed as a revised synthesis of *The Bible and Homosexual Practice*.

My first attempt at writing this essay came in at nearly 45,000 words, which then had to be pared down to meet a 15,000-word limit. Much of the material cut from the essay has been placed on my web page at www.robgagnon.net under the title "Notes to Gagnon's Essay in the Gagnon-Via *Two Views* Book." Readers do not need to consult the notes in order to make sense of this essay. However, anyone seeking further documentation of a number of points will benefit from the notes. For the convenience of such readers I have inserted note numbers at the appropriate points in this essay, corresponding to note numbers in the online notes. For example, (N1) means that the reader can find further information on this point, or on a related point, in note 1 of my online notes. The most extensive interaction with secondary literature through 1999 remains *The Bible and Homosexual Practice* (Gagnon 2001a throughout), though one will find some updating and new arguments in the notes.

The shorthand term *homosex*, in use by some "gay" publications, is employed in this essay. It has the advantage of focusing on behavior rather than orientation and can be utilized as a shorthand adjective or noun by analogy to the term *sex*. It also avoids the confusion that arises when people speak of pro- or anti-"homosexual" positions. This is not a debate about whether one should be for or against *persons* with homoerotic proclivities. The issue is willful homosexual *acts* or "homosex." In fact, withholding approval of such acts is in the best interests of those who experience homoerotic desires.

I thank Dr. Priscilla D. M. Turner for making some helpful suggestions regarding syntax and content.

I would like to dedicate my essay to Roy Harrisville III, former General Manager of Fortress Press and Augsburg Books, who at some personal risk invited me to write a procomplementarity companion piece to Dan Via's essay. His advice on how I might shorten the essay and modify it for general readership was invaluable.

This book is being brought out by the publishing house of the Evangelical Lutheran Church in America at a time when the ELCA is exploring the issue of homosexuality. It is my hope and prayer that this essay will make a positive impact on the ELCA, as elsewhere, to the glory of Christ and his church universal.

The BIBLE, the CHURCH, and HOMOSEXUALITY

DAN O. VIA

INTRODUCTION

The term "homosexual" was introduced into English from German in 1892. It is not derived from the Latin *homo* (man) but from the Greek *homoios* (like or same) and thus has to do with same-sex orientation (Edwards 1984, 14). Needless to say the church is very much divided in its judgments about this human phenomenon, so we have a topic that is delicate, sensitive, complex, divisive, and important. There are two basic positions, although each is variously nuanced. (1) The traditional view takes the Bible's strictures against homosexuality at face value. All homosexual acts are sinful by their very nature. (2) A nontraditional view seeks a more open and accepting position. Homosexual acts are not in themselves immoral or sinful but, like heterosexual acts, are good or bad depending on the context that defines and gives meaning to them. What I shall try to do in several steps is to develop a theological—in fact biblical—rationale for the second position.

1

THE AUTHORITY OF THE BIBLE

I take the Bible to be the highest authority for Christians in theological and ethical matters, although I recognize also the legitimacy of tradition, reason, and experience. Authority does not mean perfection or inerrancy or complete consistency. The authoritative norm is the one that you finally listen to in a situation of competing norms.

There are two basic views of biblical authority. (1) The *a priori* view says that the Bible is authoritative in all of its parts and is so *prior to* interpretation. Since this affirmation of total authority is made *before* one interprets the Bible—it is *assumed* before one interprets particular texts—the person who makes such an avowal must do so on the basis of someone else's opinion—a parent, pastor, or teacher's. The affirmation is not made on the ground of one's own experience. (2) The experiential or existential view says that the Bible is authoritative only in those parts that are existentially engaging and compelling—that give grounding and meaning to existence. This avowal can be made only after and in the light of one's own interpretation. At the same time it should be recognized that the Christian tradition and community are a part of the individual's location (Barr 1973, 27). I take the latter view.

HERMENEUTICS:
THE PROBLEM OF INTERPRETATION

The interpretation of a text is always strongly governed by its context, and this context is two-fold or bi-focal: (1) the literary and historical/cultural context of the text; (2) the religious, intellectual, and cultural context constituted by the interpreter's pre-understanding, presuppositions, or social location. There is no completely objective interpretation. We never have the Bible as it is in itself. We always have it from some—limited—point of view.

The church during its first few centuries—through the process of the life of faith in the real world—decided that a certain list of books was to be regarded as meaningful and authoritative. This canon (normative list) provides a rich and diverse—sometimes contradictory—context in which to try to understand individual texts. Since texts mean different things in different contexts, texts do not necessarily *mean* what they *say*. Context may positively extend the meaning of a text and provide a multiplicity of applications.

Another aspect of the text-context relationship, on the other hand, is that some larger aspect of the canonical context may simply disagree with a particular text. This generates what biblical scholars call content criticism. Does the content of a particular text agree with and do justice to the larger context of the biblical book in which it is found or the context of Scripture as a whole? Pursuing this question may lead to the conclusion that some texts are simply disqualified by the whole meaning of the gospel.

We will also want to consider our own cultural context. How does the unambiguous condemnation of homosexual acts in certain biblical texts accord with what recent social science has taught us and with the contemporary experience of gay and lesbian Christians?

CHANGING ATTITUDES

Before taking up the biblical material it might be well to look at certain trends over the last forty years or so in order to place ourselves on the spectrum of possibilities. Mark Toulouse suggests three stages or perhaps, better, positions—since all three categories can be found among contemporary Christians (Toulouse 2000, 21–24, 34–35).

1. Homosexuals as degenerates. Prior to the 1960s almost all Christians saw homosexuality as sin pure and simple, and as an individual failing.

2. Homosexuals as diseased. Mainline Protestants in the 1960s began to make a distinction between homosexual orientation (disease) and homosexual practice (sin).

3. Homosexuals as disordered. In 1974 the American Psychiatric Association dropped homosexuality from its list of mental diseases. However, the APA did recognize a category "sexual orientation disturbances," which did not include all homosexuals but designated those who were disturbed by, in conflict with, or wished to change their sexual orientation, and those who were subjectively distressed or socially impaired by their homosexuality (Edwards 1984, 16). And there have been more recent studies that some will interpret as showing that there is something pathological about homosexual orientation itself (Gagnon 2001a, 476–78).

After 1974 some mainline church leaders began to describe homosexual orientation as a disordered state with complex causes—genetic and environmental, beyond the control of the individual. A cure cannot be expected, thus some church leaders began to say that homosexuals should live out their orientation. This judgment displays the emergence of a fourth position, which, as my friend George Telford suggests, regards gay people as differently ordered rather than disordered. Toulouse opines that probably most mainline Protestants still regard homosexual behavior as sinful. The people in the muddled middle simply wish that the issue would go away. We turn now to the few biblical texts that mention homosexuality.

The Old Testament

The four pertinent Old Testament texts—two narrative and two legal—present an unambiguous and unconditional condemnation of homosexuality.

In Gen 19:1-29 two angels (male) come to Sodom, and Lot, Abraham's nephew, makes them his guests. Later the men of Sodom want to have sex with the guests, but Lot strongly resists this and offers them his two virgin daughters instead. The two angels, however, struck the men of Sodom blind and rescued Lot, his wife, and his daughters before the Lord rained destruction upon Sodom.

In a similar story in Judges 19, a Levite from Ephraim went to Bethlehem to bring back his concubine who had become angry with him and had run away. On his way back home with this woman he spent the night in Gibeah (in the territory of Benjamin) where an old man took him in as a guest. That night the men of the town want to have sex with the male guest, but the host opposed this and offered them the guest's concubine and his own virgin daughter. The concubine was actually sent out and was repeatedly raped until she died the next morning.

Let it simply be said here that these two stories have no direct bearing on the validity of contemporary consensual homosexual relationships but rather are told in such a way as to condemn homosexual gang rape. And they do, as we shall see, tell us something about how ancient Israel understood homosexuality.

Two very similar prohibitions of homosexuality appear in Lev 18:22 and 20:13—A man shall not lie with a male as with a woman. It is an abomination, and the penalty is death.

In order to grasp the context in which the Old Testament locates homosexuality we need to recognize that there are two kinds of human evil in ancient Israel—conditions and acts that are against God, create distance from the divine, and injure the human subjects: (1) sin and (2) uncleanness or impurity (Ricoeur 25–99). To which of these does homosexuality belong?

Sin is a conscious, intentional, personal attitude and act. It originates in a corrupted heart, the seat of will and understanding (Gen 3:1-7; Isa 1:2-5; Jer 7:13-14; 13:10; 17:1, 9-10). It is religious, rebellion against God (Isa 1:4; Jer 5:23). It is also moral. Since the God of Israel wills that the poor and marginalized be treated with justice and concern, rebellion against God is also an offense against one's human community (Amos 4:1; 5:11-12; 6:4-6).

Uncleanness, on the other hand, occurs from contact with some physical object or process—certain animals or foods, corpses, pagan rites, sexual processes, etc. It is like a contagion; it gets on you (Lev 15:19; Num 29:22). It has nothing to do with motive, intention, or the disposition of the heart. The only thing that matters is physical contact with the source of uncleanness. The effect is automatic. The consequence is that one may not enter the sanctuary to worship God (Lev 12:4; Num 19:13). In less serious cases sacrifice or ritual washing may remove impurity. But in the most radical cases death is required (Neusner 1973, 118; Douglas 1979, 130; Dodds 1968, 5, 34–37, 44, 48).

What is the unclean in uncleanness? What constitutes the uncleanness of the unclean object or process? The Old Testament legal traditions, and especially the Holiness Code in Leviticus 17–26, are very concerned to identify the sources of impurity and to specify the remedies, but there is no clear theory about why these things are unclean. That must be teased out by contemporary scholarship. It has been correctly denied that uncleanness in the Old Testament has to do with hygiene or physical dirt or that it is a matter of aesthetics (Neusner 1973, 1; Douglas 1979, 43, 49). It has been both denied (Douglas 1979, 43, 49) and suggested (Bird 2000, 162) that it has something to do with instinctive revulsion. A number of interesting theories have been formulated, and probably no one theory can explain all of the sources of uncleanness in the Old Testament, but I mention one that is fruitful and that seems explanatory with regard to homosexuality as a source of uncleanness.

Mary Douglas argues that the purpose of the purity rules in the Old Testament is to allow Israel to reflect in its life the holiness of God, understood as wholeness, completeness, or perfection (Douglas 1979, 43, 49, 51–52). The human body, for example, should be a perfect, unflawed, unblemished container (Douglas 1979, 51–52). That would explain why sexual emissions (Lev 15:16-30) and other bodily discharges (Lev 15:1-12) make a person unclean, as do menstruation (Lev 15:19), childbearing (Lev 12:1-5), and marital sexual intercourse (Lev 15:18). These are a breach in the body as a perfect container. A priest with bodily deformities would profane the sanctuary (Lev 21:16-24). The quest for holiness requires that individuals conform completely to the class to which they belong. Sea creatures that do not have fins and scales are unclean (Lev 11:9-12). They live in the water and thus seem to belong to the fish class, but they lack defining characteristics.

The requirement of completeness or perfection means that classes or categories must be kept distinct and not mixed, confused, or confounded. Order is required. Thus cattle are not to be bred to a different kind; fields are not to be sown with different kinds of seed; garments made of different kinds of material are not to be worn (Lev 19:19).

This means that an individual cannot belong to two different classes or enact two different fundamental roles at the same time (Soler 1979, 29–30). A person cannot be both human and animal; a man cannot be both husband and son; a man cannot be both male and female. Hence sexual intercourse with an animal (Lev 18:23), incest (Lev 18:6-18), and homosexuality (Lev 18:22; 20:13) are condemned as defiling.

In sum, the unclean in uncleanness or impurity is disorder, confusion, the mixing of what should not be mixed—a lack of the wholeness, unity, and integrity that contradicts what makes God God—holiness.

The pertinent point here is that the condemnation of homosexuality in Leviticus categorizes it as a source of uncleanness rather than as a sin. This is seen in the fact that the condemnation of homosexual practice occurs in a context in Leviticus that deals with numerous varied manifestations of impurity, including the ones mentioned in the previous paragraphs. Moreover, it specifically states that homosexuality defiles or makes unclean (Lev 18:24, 27). And homosexual practice is an "abomination" (Lev 18:22) just as eating an unclean animal or bird is an "abomination" (Lev 11:13; 20:25). The Hebrew text uses two different roots to express the idea of "abomination" in Lev 18:22, on the one hand, and in 11:13; 20:25, on the other. The two terms are synonymous, however, and the Septuagint (the Greek translation of the Old Testament) translates them both with the same Greek root.

Let me conclude the discussion of the Old Testament by indicating the ways in which the Old Testament justifies or warrants the rule against homosexual practice. Why should it not be done?

1. Homosexual practice makes one unclean—a negative mark on the person that limits one's ability to associate with other people and one's access to God.

We have seen that this is a very important category in the Old Testament, especially in the legal traditions. It is a prerational sensibility, not peculiar to Israel, whose theoretical basis is not made explicit in Scripture itself. At the same time, the judgment against homosexuality in Israel also takes on warrants that are more culturally conditioned.

2. In a patriarchal society homosexuality compromises purity in the production of male heirs to hold the land (Melcher 1996, 93–99).

3. Homosexuality violates the boundaries that separate Israel from the pagan nations (Lev 18:3, 24, 27) (Bird 2000, 151–52).

4. Homosexual practice in a patriarchal society is an affront to male honor.

This is seen especially in the two narratives. For a man to be put in the position of being the passive partner—the penetrated one—in homosexual sex is such a violation of his masculine honor that men should protect other men from this offense at almost any cost—the sacrifice of one's virgin daughters or one's concubine (Bird 2000, 147). The prevalence of this attitude across the centuries can be seen, for example, in the statement of the great fourth-century Christian preacher, John Chrysostom, that homosexuality is worse than fornication because it makes a man into a woman (Edwards 1984, 26).

At this point we might ask ourselves: Should Christians accept a rule that is justified in the way that the Old Testament justifies the condemnation of homosexuality?

TRANSITION TO THE NEW TESTAMENT

The Old Testament regards the command to avoid or to remedy uncleanness as grounded on the will of God (Lev 17:1; 18:1; 19:1; 20:1, etc.). But the New Testament annuls, delegitimizes, and invalidates in principle the very category of impurity or uncleanness. Paul is convinced that nothing is unclean in itself (Rom 14:14). He does not say that nothing is sinful but that nothing is unclean.

In Mark 7 the Pharisees criticized Jesus because some of his disciples ate with defiled hands. That is, they had presumably been out in public, may have touched something unclean, and had not performed a ritual washing. The Jesus of Mark's Gospel (scholars disagree about the position of the historical Jesus on this) responds by asserting that no physical thing can touch the heart. The physical cannot defile. Material phenomena have no defiling effect on the heart, the personal inner core, and do not disturb a person's relationship with God. What defiles is what comes from the heart—evil intentions and acts such as murder, theft, adultery, avarice, deceit, etc. So the Old Testament category of impurity is annulled. Uncleanness is not a matter of an automatic physical contagion but of a deformation of the will and understanding. Mark's Jesus reinterprets uncleanness in personal, intentional, ethical terms.

So Mark rejects the legitimacy of the *concept* of uncleanness or defilement. Contact with a physical object or process does not deform the person's heart and separate that person from God and the community. Yet Mark retains the *vocabulary* of defilement. But now it is *immoral* dispositions and acts that defile—murder, theft, deceit, and so on. It is the lack of love that comes *from* the heart that undermines the wholeness and order that purity was supposed to maintain.

When there is theological or ethical conflict within the canon, conscientious Christians simply have to decide to which side they will give priority. I choose Paul and the Gospels over Leviticus as having the more profound understanding of the human situation.

Now since the Old Testament categorizes homosexuality as a source of defilement or uncleanness—a nonintentional, automatic contagion, and since Paul and Mark delegitimize the category of uncleanness, do the two New Testament writers not implicitly annul the Old Testament condemnation of homosexuality? If, for the Christian, Mark and Paul trump Leviticus, is the biblical view of the matter not settled? Well, not really, because Paul reinterprets homosexuality as sin rather than as uncleanness. Remember, nothing is unclean for Paul, but homosexuality for him is sinful. It issues from the distorted mind and heart (Rom 1:18-28) and is personal, chosen, (im)moral, and against God. Paul brings homosexuality within the compass of the sinful and immoral and condemns it.

Is Paul arbitrary and implausible in reinterpreting homosexuality as sin? Mary Douglas states that morality and purity are quite different phenomena (Douglas 43, 49), and we have seen that sin (immorality) and uncleanness are different from each other in source and nature. But they are not totally disparate. Leviticus interweaves ethical rules—no stealing, lying, or hatred (Lev 19:11-12, 17)—with the purity rules that we have already seen, and both moral uprightness and purity are expressions of the holiness required by a holy God (Lev 19:2). The kinship between uncleanness and sin can be seen from the negative side in that just as uncleanness introduces disorder and confusion into the human enterprise, so does sin (Gen 3:14-19; Isa 1: 5-9). Moreover, the Hebrew root for abomination in Lev 18:22; 20:13 can be used in the Old Testament to express moral fault, such as murder, lying, and oppression of the poor (Jer 7:9-10; Prov 6:16-17; Ezek 16:47-52; 18:7-8; and so on; Gagnon 2001a, 119). Thus Paul's reinterpretation is not really arbitrary. But we must still pursue the question of whether Paul's *ethical* rule (at least an implicit rule) against homosexual practice is finally justifiable in light of the larger canonical message of redemption.

THE NEW TESTAMENT

There are two pertinent New Testament texts, both in Paul (1 Cor 6:9-10; Rom 1:21-27). In 1 Cor 6:9-10 Paul lists several kinds of wrongdoers who will not inherit the kingdom of God—adulterers, thieves, the greedy, etc. Among these sinners Paul includes two others that the New Revised Standard Version translates as male prostitutes (*malakoi*) and sodomites (*arsenokoitai*).

It should be kept in mind that scholars tend to agree that male homosexuality in the ancient Greek world was primarily, if not exclusively, a matter of pederasty—a relationship between an adult male and a boy. The Pauline texts, however, do not support this limitation of male homosexuality to pederasty. Moreover, some Greek sources suggest that—at least in principle—a relationship should not be begun until the boy is almost grown and should be lifelong (see the speech of Pausanias in Plato, *Symposium*, 181cde, 183de).

The basic denotation of *malakos* is "soft." It is not unusual for scholars to see this term as a reference to the passive (young) partner in a homosexual relationship, and this interpretation is possibly, if not probably, correct (Barrett 1968, 140; Conzelmann 1975, 106; Waetjen 1996, 109–10). But *malakos* (soft one) is not a technical—or the ordinary—term for the passive partner (Hays 1997, 97), and this word had many connotations. It could refer to the softness of expensive clothes, the delicacy of gourmet food, or the gentleness of a light breeze. In a moral context it connoted something perceived as soft—laziness or cowardice. Dale Martin holds that the governing connotation is the feminine, or when applied to men, effeminate. It could refer to the passive, penetrated partner in male homosexual intercourse, or it could refer to men who enjoyed women too much or who prettied themselves up excessively to further their heterosexual exploits (Martin 1996, 124–28).

Martin, again, argues that being penetrated was negatively evaluated as inferior because it was typically women who were penetrated and a patriarchal society regarded women as inferior (Martin 1996, 127–29). Perhaps it was in reaction to the attribution of feminine inferiority to male homosexuality that Pausanias maintained that when a male is attracted to the male he is attracted to what is naturally stronger and of superior intelligence (Plato, *Symposium*, 181c). And Aristophanes similarly asserted that males who pursue males are the best and the most manly. They are not immoral but are rather boldly courageous since they take pleasure in what is like themselves (Plato, *Symposium*, 191e, 192a).

The second pertinent term in 1 Cor 6:9-10 (found also in 1 Tim 1:10)—*arsenokoitēs*—is often taken to refer to the active partner in male homosexuality (Barrett 140; Conzelmann 106; Waetjen 109–10). This term does not occur in Greek literature prior to Paul (Hays 1997, 97), and there are rather few uses of it at all. Therefore, Martin is dubious about our attaining any certainty regarding its meaning. He leans to the idea that it means exploiting others by means of sex (Martin 1996, 123).

I believe that Hays is correct in holding that *arsenokoitēs* refers to a man who engages in same-sex intercourse (Hays 1997, 97). The term is a compound of the words for "male" (*arsēn*) and "bed" (*koitē*) and thus could naturally be taken to mean a man who goes to bed with other men. True the meaning of a compound word does not necessarily add up to the sum of its parts (Martin 119). But in this case I believe the evidence suggests that it does. In the Greek version of the two Leviticus passages that condemn male homosexuality (Lev 18:22; 20:13)—a man is not to lie with a male as with a woman—each text contains both the words *arsēn* and *koitē*. First Cor 6:9-10 simply classifies homosexuality as a moral sin that finally keeps one out of the kingdom of God. The Romans text carries a more probing analysis.

The verses in Romans that treat homosexuality (1:24-27) occur in a context (1:18-32) dealing with the wrath of God, not as the final judgment (as in 2:5-6), but as the anticipation of that final judgment, which happens regularly throughout the historical process. The theological horizon of Paul's discourse here is that God has made knowledge and truth about God's self available to all people in the created world (1:19-20). But human beings in their foolish and willful self-interest have rejected this truth (1:18, 21, 25) and therefore exist with minds that are dark, senseless, and futile (1:21-22). God's reaction to this universal rebellion—God's wrath—is that God turns people over to the consequences of their own action. God darkens the human mind (1:21b, 28b). God ratifies the foolish human choice. Thus the state of obdurate hostility to God in which humankind lives is— in accord with the characteristic biblical paradox—a matter of both human choice and divine determination. And that is true of homosexuality in particular. It is something to which people are given over by God and which is also chosen by human beings.

One of the conditions to which God's wrath gives people up is homosexual relations (1:24, 26), and Paul includes both women and men in this text. All of the Old Testament texts have only men in view. Thus here in Romans same-sex relations are not so much sin itself—or at least *the* sin—as the consequence of sin, what God gives people up to. And yet it is sin because it is a chosen behavior (1:25-27). Given what we now know about the genetic, social, and psychological causes of homosexuality, and the graciousness of God's creative intention (see below), it is difficult to accept Paul's view that universal human rebellion and God's wrath, in their mutual interaction, are the primary cause of homosexuality. And yet there may be a valid underlying principle implied here: the deep wellsprings of all sexuality are deformed by human rebellion against God's truth.

In the Greco-Roman world of Paul's time there were non-Christian moralists who defended homosexuality and those who opposed it (Scroggs 1983, 44–65; Furnish 1979, 62–66). Paul's critical description of same-sex relations agrees essentially with the non-Christian opponents.

Paul ascribes impurity to same-sex relations (1:24), but it is clear in context that he means impurity reinterpreted as sin and not impurity in the Old Testament sense. More to the point, he traces homosexual relations to excessive lust—they were consumed with passion; yet he regards homosexuality as chosen—they exchanged natural for unnatural relations (1:26-27). And perhaps most importantly he regards same-sex relations as contrary to nature (1:26-27), contrary to the order of the world as created by God.

These statements prompt critical questions. Are homosexuals as a whole more consumed with lust than heterosexuals? In view of the high probability of the reality of a homosexual orientation, can we think of homosexuality as simply chosen? And what about "contrary to nature"?

HOMOSEXUAL ORIENTATION

Paul seems to have agreed with the generally held belief of the ancient world that there is only one sexual nature, what we would call a heterosexual nature. Therefore, what he is condemning as contrary to nature is homosexual acts by people with a heterosexual nature. His implied underlying principle is that if people choose to actualize their sexuality, their acts should be in accord with their nature or orientation. If Paul then could be confronted with the reality of homosexual orientation, consistency would require him to acknowledge the naturalness of homosexual acts for people with a homosexual orientation.

Christine Gudorf strikes a frequently heard note when she states that the most fundamental insight of recent social science regarding homosexuality is the discovery of sexual orientation (2000, 122). Richard Hays (1996, 388), for example, reflects that position when he states that neither Paul nor anyone else in the ancient world had a concept of sexual orientation. It should be observed, however, that in certain—perhaps small—circles in the ancient Mediterranean world there was some awareness of a homosexual disposition or orientation (see Schoedel 2000, 46–47; Gagnon 2001a, 384–85). Aristophanes, for example, speaking in Plato's *Symposium,* affirms that our original human nature was quite different from what it is now. In the original time there were three sexes: male, female, and a combination sex comprising both male and female and called hermaphrodite. The original beings made an assault on the gods, so Zeus decided to weaken them by cutting each of them in two. As a result, each half went around looking for its other half. Those men derived from a half of the original male are attracted to men of the other male half. And the same is true for women—like attracted to like. But men who are fragments of the combination or hermaphrodite sex are attracted to women of the female half, and women of the combination sex are attracted to men. Aristophanes tends to take a dim view of the descendants of the combination sex. Most of the men seem to be womanizers and the women nymphomaniacs (Plato, *Symposium*, 189de, 190bc, 191ade).

Aristophanes' words represent a mythological—though clearly not a scientific—awareness of something like sexual orientation. The several kinds of sexuality contemplated by Plato's Aristophanes—male homosexuality, female homosexuality, male and female heterosexuality—were generated by a divine act that belonged to the original time preceding the emergence of humankind as we know it. This act, which produced human beings as they now exist, in fact formed the boundary between original time and "our" time. Thus whatever kind of sexuality one has results from a divinely determined—unchosen—predisposition.

Robert Gagnon thinks it likely that Paul was familiar with one or more of the ancient theories about a congenital homosexual nature or orientation (20001, 385). I do not believe that there is clear evidence that Paul had such knowledge. If, however, he did in fact know about and believe in some kind of homosexual nature or orientation, he could not *with logical consistency* have said that homosexual practice was against nature. He logically should have acknowledged the naturalness of it.

To return to present usage, sexual *orientation* means a *proclivity* or predisposition that is given and not deliberately chosen or subject to the will of the individual. Sexual orientations exist on a spectrum that stretches between exclusively heterosexual and exclusively homosexual individuals (Gudorf 2000, 122). There are differing degrees of homosexuality. Kinsey found, for example, that 37 percent of males between adolescence and old age had at least some homosexual experience to the point of orgasm, but only 4 percent were exclusively homosexual throughout life (Edwards 1984, 17). Sexual orientation is fixed relatively early in life. There is controversy over whether an orientation once fixed is ever open to reversal. But there is general agreement that at the very least it is extremely resistant to change even among highly motivated people (Gudorf 2000, 122–23). From the evidence of homosexual orientation, Gudorf (140) concludes that the church should recognize homosexual marriage. It would serve the same purpose that heterosexual marriage serves for Paul—protection against the temptation to promiscuity (1 Cor 7:2, 9).

An essentialist view of sexual orientation holds that homosexuality is innate, biologically or genetically caused, while a constructionist interpretation maintains that it results from the interaction of psychological and social forces on the person. There would appear to be evidence for both positions (Gudorf 124).

Studies on homosexual and heterosexual persons who are not psychiatric patients suggest that there are no significant differences between the two with regard to psychological health, criminality, dependability, or social responsibility. This implies that homosexuality in itself is not pathological (Gudorf 128). It also suggests that homosexual practice need not injure—deform the hearts—of those involved.

Should Christians who are looking for a theological basis for an appropriate ethical posture toward homosexuality take seriously the claims of scientific studies that homosexual orientation is a reality and should they draw ethical consequences from it? There is a strand in the Bible, especially in the Wisdom tradition, which attests that the natural world and human nature and experience are possible clues to knowledge of God and of moral propriety (Ps 19:1-2; Rom 1:19-20; 2:14-15; Acts 10:34-35). One of the tasks of the Wisdom teacher was to observe and study the natural world for evidence of God (1 Kgs 4:32-33; Wis 7:15-22; Sir 38:1-8) (Gudorf 2000, 135; Bird 2000, 168). Modern science with its own technical method studies nature, not for evidence of God, but simply to understand the world. But the Bible itself implies that some findings of science may be recontextualized and made theologically and ethically useful, for science is the technical extension of the Wisdom teacher's observations of nature. This is not to say that all science will be useful; and scientific claims, like all other human claims, are always subject to questioning and revision. But the Bible allows that in principle scientific understanding may be theologically germane. Moreover, the gospel calls on believers to be faithful in the particular culture in which they are placed by God. Thus the church should listen—critically and in light of its own theological horizon—to the best cultural voices.

DEFENSE OF THE TRADITIONAL POSITION

In recent years the church's traditional position has been defended by knowledgeable and competent scholars. I give three representative examples. Stanton L. Jones and Mark A. Yarhouse have taken a thorough look at both the scientific literature on the subject and a number of nontraditional positional documents from mainline denominations. These authors argue in favor of the traditional Christian position that the revealed will of God allows only two sexual alternatives—heterosexual marriage or celibacy outside of marriage. All homosexual acts are immoral by their very nature, in themselves (2000a, 73–74, 118–19).

For the Jones-Yarhouse position it is only the acts that are to be considered in assessing the moral justifiability of homosexual practice—and also decisive is the implied biblical rule pertaining to the act: homosexual practice is forbidden in all circumstances. It does not matter if the relationship is grounded on love and is nonpromiscuous and nonexploitative. The integrated wholeness of the persons involved does not count. Nor do intentions and consequences have any bearing on the question. None of these factors is allowed to qualify this act or to neutralize its (alleged) wrongness (2000a, 73, 82).

The authors believe that the findings of science do not clearly support the ethical conclusions that the nontraditionalists draw from this scientific evidence (74, 118). Jones and Yarhouse do in fact acknowledge such a thing as sexual orientation. They concede that genetic factors, brain structure, and prenatal hormonal causation seem to "push" some subpopulation of persons into a proclivity for homosexuality. But social and psychological factors must also be taken into account. And the reality of such a proclivity does not rule out the role of human choice (90, 104–6). These considerations seem to lead Jones and Yarhouse to the conclusion that homosexual orientation is difficult to change; change is not a likely prospect but is nevertheless not impossible. All studies of change from homosexual to heterosexual orientation claim some—even if slight—success. Homosexuality is not absolutely immutable (2000a, 112–14).

One of the valuable things about the Jones-Yarhouse article is that it so sharply focuses the difference between the traditional and nontraditional positions. For Jones and Yarhouse, in the long run, science is accorded only a very marginal role in Christian ethical reflection. Even if it could be definitively shown by science that homosexuality is common, utterly unassociated with psychological distress, genetically caused, and utterly unchangeable, the traditional position would have to engage ethical and theological—not scientific—grounds (2000a, 118–20).

This is to deny that our social/cultural context and the knowledge gained from it have any significant part in deciding about ethical issues. I have two reactions:

1. To limit ethical discussion to acts and rules, to the exclusion of consequences, intentions, and inner dispositions, is a reductionist version of ethical discourse. I note particularly that the exclusive focus on acts has the effect of nullifying the category of character—the gestalt of inner dispositions or the encompassing thrust of the whole self. Persons are reduced to strings of acts—good and bad—and no cognizance is taken of a total ordered self or wholeness to which acts are related. The heart as the essential unifying self is ignored. This is contrary to important

New Testament strands, in which character or selfhood and actions affect each other reciprocally. According to Mark 9:43-48, character or the whole self is represented by the personal "you," while specific acts that you may perform are symbolized by parts of the body—hand, foot, eye. Conduct affects character. A sinful act causes *you* to sin. The whole self participates in the act and is deformed by it. At the same time character shapes conduct. *You* can and should terminate or reverse the sinful acts and thereby recover your self. Character has power to transform conduct. The command to amputate the sinning member—hand, foot, or eye—should not be taken literally. That would not address the problem at issue here, namely, the relationship between act and the whole inner self, the heart (Mark 7:18-23). In Matt 7:17-18; 12:33-35; 23:26 you cannot get bad fruit from a good tree, that is, bad acts or words from a good heart. So if the heart is loving, the acts that flow from it cannot be evil, though this is a principle that cannot be absolutized. The inner nature of a homosexual relationship does qualify the acts.

2. From the few biblical texts dealing with homosexuality Jones and Yarhouse have derived an ethical rule: homosexual practice is prohibited in all circumstances. They have then separated this rule from all of its contextual horizons. They have abstracted the rule from its literary and social-historical contexts in the Bible. They have severed act from character or heart. They have detached the rule from the impact of the conditions and knowledge of our present cultural setting.

It should be made very clear here that this choice to absolutize the rule and to nullify the force of context—a position also taken essentially by Hays and Gagnon—is a philosophical decision that is logically prior to taking a position about same-sex relations and is a move not required by the Bible itself. It is a position one brings to the Bible. Following helpful leads from Gene Outka's discussion (Outka 1972, 94, 103, 114–16), I suggest that there are four possible positions that one may take regarding the relationship between rules and the possible normative signals from contexts of various kinds:

1. Rules have no validity.
2. Rules are useful, but if there is a conflict between rule and context, the rule can simply be discarded.
3. If there is such a conflict, the rule cannot simply be discarded, but there may be certain contextual factors which are weighty enough to override the rule.
4. There are no contextual situations that could override a rule forbidding an act that the rule, by prior determination, has designated as intrinsically immoral.

Jones and Yarhouse take the fourth position. I take the third one because I believe that it is the most inclusive and circumspect, taking serious account of both factors. If one takes this way, it can lead to two different conclusions. (1) There are factors that can justify overriding the rule in certain specific situations, but this does not invalidate the rule in principle. It retains its authority, and one is guilty for breaking it although that was the best thing in the situation. (2) There are other cases in which comprehensive contextual factors are powerful enough to invalidate the rule in principle. With regard to many issues I would take the first of these, but with respect to homosexuality I will argue for the second.

Richard Hays, in his much-acclaimed *The Moral Vision of the New Testament,* also defends the traditional Christian view. He points out that Scripture consistently and unconditionally condemns homosexuality and represents heterosexual marriage as the only justifiable expression of sexuality (Hays 1996, 381–82, 389–91), and Hays's discussion disallows that there are any interpretive moves that can legitimately override this condemnation. Hays seems to feel that the Bible's *unanimous* opposition to homosexual practice gives to this position a special force (389). There is, however, no a priori reason why a univocal position cannot be overridden if the countervailing biblical, theological, and cultural considerations have sufficient strength, as I believe they do.

Hays correctly points out that Paul's denunciation of homosexuality in Romans 1 is contextualized in the symbolic world of universal human sinfulness and confusion that arouse the divine wrath. Homosexual practice is contrary to the will of God in that it is a violation of nature, a transgression against God's creative design for the world (Hays 1996, 386–87). And Hays believes that this picture should be taken seriously as revealed reality (396). But in 1 Cor 11:14 Paul also claims that nature correctly teaches proper hairstyle. If nature, as God's design, gives authoritative directions about allowable sexual behavior, does Hays want to regard also the directions about proper hairstyle as authoritative revelation?

According to Hays, Paul articulates no clear *rule* against homosexual practice (but Paul does state a concise rule against fornication in 1 Cor 6:18), and we therefore should not derive a rule from the Pauline texts (1996, 394). If we are to use New Testament texts normatively for ethics, we should let the texts function in the mode in which they speak, and there are two modes spoken in the Romans and 1 Corinthians texts. The first is the evocation of a symbolic world: humankind in rebellion against God and subject to the divine wrath. The second is a moral principle, which could be interpreted in various ways: human actions ought to acknowledge and honor God as creator. Read against the background of the Genesis creation story, Paul concludes from this principle that homosexual practice is contrary to the will of God (Hays 1996, 394–96).

Does Hays in fact extract a rule from Paul—and the Old Testament? I believe that he does. His rule is implicit rather than explicitly and concisely stated, and it is derived from a symbolic world and an ethical principle, but a rule so expressed and derived is still a rule. That is, it is a normative position conveying that a specific or particular behavior ought or ought not be done. Hays's implicit rule is: homosexual practice is forbidden for Christians. And the rule is unexceptionable: it is forbidden in all situations (1996, 390–91, 394–95, 401). Therefore, my critique of Jones and Yarhouse with regard to the rule-and-context issue is applicable also to Hays.

Apropos of Hays's normative affirmation of the understanding of God's design for the world (nature) in Romans 1, it should be noted that at points the canon gives us permission to question other canonical interpretations of God's design for the world and the moral governance of it. In the book of Job the hero is pictured as right in questioning the moral order of the human world. Job refuses to concede that the righteous prosper and the wicked suffer. In taking that position he is brought into opposition with a significant segment of biblical material—the Deuteronomic history and much Wisdom teaching. Ecclesiastes begins on the note that all is vanity (1:2), questions whether we live in a moral universe (4:1-4), and doubts that we can discern God's design for the world and history (3:11; 8:17; 11:5) (see Bird 2000, 168–69). Paul's interpretation of God's creative design is subject to critical reinterpretation.

On the basis of his interpretation of the biblical material Hays believes that Christians with a homosexual orientation should abstain from homosexual practice and that the church should not sanction or bless gay and lesbian unions. He also holds, on the other hand, that the church should support civil rights for homosexuals, should welcome gays and lesbians into the church along with other sinners, and should not deny ordination to nonpracticing homosexuals. At the same time, Hays believes that the church should challenge self-defined homosexuals to reshape their identity in conformity with the gospel and apparently believes that such change is possible (1996, 400–404).

It may well be that some homosexuals can change without undue distress, but uncertainty about the percentage of homosexuals for whom that is true makes it an inappropriate principle for determining the general posture of the church toward gay people.

Hays takes cognizance of the concept of sexual orientation but makes no positive use of it. He states that to use it in interpreting Rom 1:24-27 is anachronistic, for it somehow suggests that Paul was aware of the idea (1996, 388–89). But in my interpretation of that passage above I neither assumed nor implied that Paul knew about a homosexual orientation, quite the contrary. He probably assumed one human nature, what we would call heterosexual. I was critically assessing Paul in light of a recent concept that for us has a high degree of probability. That is no more anachronistic than criticizing the Genesis creation chronology or flat earth assumption in the light of modern geology and astronomy.

Hays then argues that even if same-sex attraction could be proved to be essential and genetically programmed, that would not necessarily make homosexual behavior morally appropriate. Surely Christian ethics does not want to hold, he says, that all inborn traits are good and desirable. Take the analogy of alcoholism, which is generally considered to be an innate predisposition (1996, 397–98). Hays clearly regards homosexual practice as sinful, and by making homosexuality analogous to alcoholism he is also implying that it is harmful or injurious. Everyone knows that it is harmful for an alcoholic to drink. But that begs the question, for the question at issue is precisely whether homosexual practice is in fact harmful in itself.

Hays is saying in effect that homosexual practice is to homosexual orientation as drinking is to alcoholism. So homosexual practice is harmful. For Paul sin is harmful by its very nature. Sin and injury are organically united. Sin distorts and deforms both the inner life and communal life of both sinner and sinned-against (Rom 1:21-23, 28-32; 5:12; 7:5, 9-24; 1 Cor 6:18; 8:9-13). Paul is so tightly bound to the Jewish (and some Greco-Roman) judgment of his time that homosexuality is sinful, and he so inseparably connects sin and injury that he assumed homosexuality to be harmful (Rom 1:24-27). But that is an assumption that needs to be tested by the experience and knowledge of our time. If it cannot be demonstrated that homosexual practice is harmful in itself—in mutual, consensual, committed relationships—then it cannot be shown, in Pauline terms, that it is sinful. It is abundantly clear that dreadful damage to health—physical and psychological—is produced by promiscuous gay sex (Gagnon 2001a, 471–76). In no way am I defending that behavior. I am rather seeking to articulate a theological justification for homosexual practice in consensual, committed, loving relationships. Such couples undoubtedly do not compose an impressively large population in our time, but that is not a moral reason to throw them to the wind.

Robert Gagnon's *The Bible and Homosexual Practice* treats all of the biblical texts that deal directly or indirectly with homosexuality, as well as pertinent ancient Near Eastern and Greek material and contemporary social-scientific, psychiatric, and theological-ethical discussions that bear on the hermeneutical dimension of the issue. The objective of his book is two-fold: (1) to define same-sex intercourse unequivocally as sin; (2) to show that there are no hermeneutical or contextual considerations, or any aggregation of such, from either the first century or the twenty-first, that can override the biblical position against homosexual practice (Gagnon 2001a, 37, 341–493).

The concept of homosexual orientation needs a bit more attention. Gagnon recognizes the reality of this orientation and holds that it arises from the complex interplay of biological-genetic factors, social-psychological-environmental factors, and choice. The biological is not dominant and does not constitute a determinism (38, 401, 413, 418, 430). Although it is difficult for people with a homosexual orientation to change to a heterosexual one, it is possible for at least some of them (426, 428). Gagnon does acknowledge that empirically not all homosexuals *will* change and that some Christians who have apparently made a sincere effort to make this change have not been able to do it (428–29).

This acknowledgment, however, does not lead Gagnon to qualify in any way the Bible's unconditional prohibition of same-sex intercourse. He sees the urges present in homosexual orientation as a strand in what Paul grasps as the power of sin (Rom 5:12-21; 7:7-23; 8:1-7) (430–31). This is a negative theological interpretation of homosexual orientation, and it is correct in the sense that—just like heterosexual desire—it can be pursued in evil, destructive, exploitative ways. But that does not demonstrate that homosexual orientation as such, or its practice, is evil in itself. As I shall try to show, homosexual orientation can be placed in an understanding of creation—instead of sin—and given a positive interpretation.

At the end of the day, for Gagnon Scripture allows only two sexual alternatives: (1) monogamous heterosexual marriage, and (2) celibacy (432).

The reasons why Christians should oppose homosexual practice are primarily two. The main reason is the revelatory authority of the Bible (40). The second reason is that same-sex intercourse is contrary to nature. It is contrary to nature in the sense of God's design for the relationship of the sexes. This design is *revealed* by *God* and *attested* in *Scripture*. But it is manifested in the material creation—visibly and palpably—and is not distorted or corrupted by the fall. It is seen in the complementarity or compatibility of the male and female sex organs, which includes the anatomical fittedness of penis and vaginal receptacle, the procreative function, and the capacity for mutual and pleasurable stimulation. Same-sex intercourse violates the otherness or difference that belongs to sexual relations in God's creative intent (40–41, 138–42, 254–62, 380, 392). Gagnon sounds this note with great regularity throughout the book and uses it as his most frequent argument in support of unconditional rejection of homosexual practice in both Testaments.

I will respond to the first of Gagnon's two reasons here and to the second one in the last section of this piece. Gagnon would undoubtedly defend his absolutizing of the biblical prohibition of all same-sex intercourse on the ground that it is in fact *revealed* in *Scripture*. I have shown, however, and will show that there are *biblical* themes, as well as extra-biblical horizons, that *countervail against* this biblical proscription. But Gagnon—like Jones and Yarhouse and Hays—does not grant to the opposing biblical material the same authority that he grants to the rule against same-sex intercourse. This shows that the final authority for these scholars is not Scripture itself. It is rather the prior philosophical position that they bring to Scripture (a hermeneutical lens), namely, the position that there are no contextual factors that can override a rule forbidding an act that the rule, by prior determination, has designated as intrinsically immoral. If these scholars do not take this position with regard to other ethical issues, it is unknown why they take it with regard to homosexuality.

Although Gagnon has dealt with homosexual orientation, he states that his *focus* on homosexual acts, as opposed to homosexual orientation, reflects the Bible's own relative lack of interest in the motives or originations of same-sex impulses (37–38). To make this move, however, is to instantiate the gay phenomenon in the realm of unclean/clean rather than in the realm of sin/righteousness (the moral realm), where Paul has correctly put it, even if we must raise critical questions about the specific thrust of Paul's theological-ethical discourse on this issue. That is to say, it is precisely the concept of the unclean that regards certain objects, processes, and actions as manifesting a kind of contagion that automatically contaminates without regard for motives or intentions. Gagnon's assimilation of homosexual practice to the unclean brings him into conflict with those important strands in both testaments that maintain the reciprocal interaction between actions and the dispositions of the heart. To ignore the latter is to have a reduced view of the structure of human existence.

Moreover, for Gagnon, as we have seen, one of the chief faults in homosexual practice is that it involves the *blurring* of the sexes—the failure to keep categories distinct (349). This shows that Gagnon, despite himself, edges same-sex intercourse out of the range of sin and into the range of uncleanness. That is, the confounding of categories *is* the unclean thing in uncleanness. I believe that Gagnon takes a misstep here. If homosexual practice is to be discussed in a Christian context as culpable in all cases, it should be articulated as sin and not as uncleanness—because the New Testament has delegitimized the latter category.

Regarding the institutional posture of the church toward homosexuals, Gagnon believes that it should love and minister to them and hold membership and church office open to celibate homosexuals, and it should be repeatedly forgiving to those who backslide and repent. At the same time discipline should be exercised toward those who indefinitely refuse to repent of homosexual acts, and the church should not bless gay unions (489–91).

WANDERING IN THE WILDERNESS

The church is in a time of conflict and uncertainty regarding the question of homosexuality. There are sharp differences between traditionalists and nontraditionalists. There are differences about the nature of biblical authority, differences about how to deal with conflicts within the canon, differences about the operation of the hermeneutical circle. There are conflicts among competent scholars about whether homosexual orientation is essential or constructed and about whether any homosexuals can change. And as I am trying to show, more than one position can be derived from Scripture.

Phyllis Bird (2000, 169–70) has suggested that the story of Israel's wandering in the wilderness is an appropriate metaphor for our situation of conflict and uncertainty. Israel has been lib-

erated from Egyptian slavery but has not yet reached the prom-
ised land.

Israel is in the wilderness and is afraid to try to capture the land
that God wants to give them, for that would be too dangerous. It
would be better to go back to Egyptian slavery than to trust God
to give them an unknown future of freedom. There are differences of opinion about what to do. Then as punishment for not
having the capacity to trust what God has in store in the unseen
beyond, Israel is forced to wander for forty years in the wilderness
(Exod 14:12; Num 13:20—14:4; 14:8-13, 15-16, 19, 22-23, 33).

On the issue of the moral legitimacy of homosexual practice,
the church is in the wilderness. It seems to me that there is too
much against the traditional view to stay in the Egyptian box, but
we are less than certain about the future. The exodus and wilderness stories are told in such a way as to urge strongly that the people of God should look forward to a new future and not return to
the security of an enslaving past. Don't go back to Egypt.

A WAY FORWARD

How might Scripture, reason, and experience lead the church to
a new, nontraditional understanding of the moral justifiability of
homosexual practice? The evidence of reason—science—and
experience is relevant and important; but Christians who want to
take an open, nontraditional position on this should be able to
find biblical support for it. Of course, the few biblical texts that
deal explicitly with the subject offer no such support. But all
interpretation is from a point of view, a question. If we look
broadly at Scripture, what does it yield if we ask the question:
What does the creative and redemptive purpose of God and the
ethic of love tell the church its posture should be toward homosexual practice—assuming that the relationship is loving, consensual, nonmanipulative, and faithful?

1. In the Bible human existence is essentially bodily. The self is defined and constituted by the body. This is very different from the Platonic and broadly Greek view that the essential self is a soul or spirit encased in a body that is regarded as inferior or evil. For the Bible, the essential self is an enlivened, vitalized body. I give two textual examples.

In the earlier of the two creation stories (Gen 2:7) God formed humankind from the earth, blew life into him/her, and they became living souls. The soul is not something separate or separable from the body but is in fact the vitalized body. We should, of course, not think of this story as historically or literally true, but I take it to be representative of the general biblical view and to be existentially true. It is a true image of the nature of human existence.

In 1 Corinthians Paul can speak of the believer's relationship with the risen Christ as both a bodily (6:13, 15) and a spiritual (6:17) connection. This suggests that for Paul, at least in certain contexts, body and spirit are interchangeable terms. Each is an aspect of the whole person; each represents the whole. Body and spirit are not separable parts of the person. The human spirit is not some kind of rarefied substance enclosed in the body. It is rather the capacity of the body to know itself and surrounding reality (1 Cor 2:10-11; 16:18; 2 Cor 2:13; 7:13) and to be open to God (Rom 8:16). And body is thus the concrete specificity in which this knowing openness is structured (see Via 1990, 68–73).

2. This bodily existence is sexually defined. Richard Hays declares that never does Scripture make sexuality the basis for defining a person's identity or for finding meaning and fulfillment in life (1996, 391). In view of the exaggerated tendency of our culture to make sexuality *the* defining feature of being human, his statement is understandable and has a certain point, but it is an overstatement. In the Bible sexuality is *a* defining feature of human being.

The later creation story states that God made humankind in

God's image and that this image exists as male and female (Gen 1:26-27). Male and female are united as human and differentiated as sexual (Trible 15–18). Human being as bodily is sexually defined. The earlier creation story declares that husband and wife become one flesh (Gen.2:24), and this is reaffirmed in the New Testament (Mark 10:6-8). Note that the Gospel of Mark does not base the indissolubility of marriage on the oneness of heart and spirit but on the oneness of flesh. To be human is to be sexual, and this is a reality that belongs to the defining structure of human existence (Mauser 1996, 5).

Paul believed that marriage was a second-best alternative to celibacy (1 Cor 7:1-2, 7-8, 28b, 32-33). Therefore, it is extraordinary that he fully recognizes the reality and legitimacy of sexual desire in both male and female. Both husband and wife are to render to the other her or his sexual rights and are not to deprive each other except for mutually agreed upon periods of prayer (1 Cor 7:3, 5). Admittedly, Paul sees this arrangement as an antidote to promiscuity (1 Cor 7:2, 5); but the important point here is that he does legitimize sexual desire in itself and makes no appeal to the intention to procreate as the only moral justification for marital sexual intercourse.

This distinguishes Paul from Plato, and from other Greco-Roman and Jewish moralists. For Plato the purpose of marriage is to benefit the state—to produce children for the state—and not to please oneself (*Laws* 721ab, 772de, 773b). Sexual intercourse is warranted only within marriage, and only when married people have intercourse in order to procreate is the pleasure "according to nature." Homosexuality in both sexes is "contrary to nature"— it cannot produce children and is solely for pleasure—and evidently so is marital sexual intercourse contrary to nature when it is engaged in simply for pleasure (*Laws* 636c, 838e, 839ab, 841de). The force of pleasure should be kept out of gear as far as possible (*Laws* 839a, 841a), for to fail in the battle with pleasure is to undermine bliss (840c).

The first-century C.E. Stoic, Musonius Rufus, agrees with Plato. Homosexuality is monstrously contrary to nature. And heterosexual intercourse is justified only within marriage and only for the purpose of procreation. Even marital intercourse that is only for pleasure is unjust and manifests a lack of self-restraint (see Malherbe 1986, 152–53). In comparison with Plato and Musonius Rufus, Paul is a virtual liberal.

But the discussion up to this point has had to do with the legitimacy of heterosexual practice in the Bible. Sexual desire is a part of being human, and in marriage each partner has an obligation to meet the sexual needs of the other. On what grounds could this legitimation of sexual practice be extended to gay and lesbian relationships? This is where rational scientific knowledge comes in. Recall that the Bible justifies in principle a critical use of scientific knowledge in theological-ethical discourse.

3. *Gay and lesbian persons are also bodily and sexual.* They differ from heterosexuals in that their sexual desire is for someone of the same sex. We do not know for certain whether homosexual orientation is essential (biological and genetic) or constructed (psychological and social) or both; but whatever is the case, even some who hold very strongly to the traditional view agree that at least some part of the gay population is immutably so.

I am sure that most heterosexuals experience their sexual orientation as something given, something they did not choose. It is an inalienable part of their existence. Christian heterosexuals will believe that their orientation was given by God as a part of the creation of the world (Gen 1:26-27; 2:24; Mark 10:6-9) and thus as being natural (Rom 1:26-27), in accord with God's creative intention for the world.

The heterosexual's orientation may be understood, and is understood in the Bible, as a destiny that is an integral part of God's creative intention. John Macquarrie defines destiny as a goal that is experienced as having been set by some transhuman agency. Destiny does not necessarily rule out freedom, for one may choose and struggle to fulfill one's destiny (Macquarrie 1986, 153).

Somewhat more elaborately, for Paul Tillich destiny is myself as given, the concrete set of circumstances that have formed me through nature, history, and my own actions. Freedom is exercised by deliberating about the possibilities offered by these particular circumstances, selecting some and cutting off others, and holding myself responsible for my decisions. Destiny then is not the opposite of freedom but is the concrete set of circumstances out of which decisions arise. At the same time destiny conditions and limits freedom, for it does not offer infinite possibilities (Tillich 1951, 201–6).

Destiny is the opportunity to act in freedom and also a limitation on that freedom. One cannot choose concrete possibilities that one does not have. Heterosexual orientation is a destiny in this sense. The orientation imposes a limit, for a heterosexual person cannot *not be* heterosexual (although, of course, one can act against one's orientation). But this person has a number of possibilities to choose among in freedom for the actualization of the orientation in practice. The Bible regards the actualization of heterosexual orientation as legitimate in principle.

The gay person is in an analogous situation. His/her orientation is a destiny that both affords and limits freedom. This person cannot *not be* homosexual (there may be exceptions), but being gay offers various concrete possibilities to choose among in freedom for actualizing this destiny. Since the homosexual is for Christian faith as much a part of God's creation as the heterosexual, how can the homosexual destiny, which is as inalienable as the heterosexual destiny, not be regarded as a part of God's creative intent, just as the heterosexual destiny is so regarded? The orientation in both cases is inalienable. And why should the homosexual, in contrast to the heterosexual, be singled out as not having the moral freedom to actualize the only orientation he/she has?

I believe that there are theological-ethical grounds for not imposing on homosexual orientation either of the negative judgments mentioned in the previous paragraph—not a part of God's creative intent and not permitted actualization. There are grounds that support the justifiability of responsible, faithful, homosexual practice.

4. *Human life is bodily and sexual, and all human lives are God's own, loved by God* (John 1:3, 11; 3:16). There is nothing that God did not bring into being through God's revealing and redemptive Word, who became incarnate in Jesus. Human life is bodily and sexual, and God wants every person to have life that is abundant, remarkable, extraordinary (John 10:10). The Gospel of John uses the expressions life, abundant life, and eternal life interchangeably. To have life is to be open to God and Jesus and to exist from them (5:24; 17:3), and this issues in a dimension of life that is qualitatively different from the ordinary life of this world. The idea of eternal life in John takes its origin from the Jewish idea of the world to come, the new age that will follow this world in the future. The important thing that distinguishes John from Judaism is the affirmation that life, abundant life, eternal life has become a reality here and now in this world through the coming of Jesus (3:36; 5:24; 6:47, 54; 11:25-26) (Dodd 1953, 144–50; Bultmann 1955, 19–20). For the believer and in the believing community things are radically different.

Human life is bodily and sexual, and God wants all of God's human creations to have life in abundance. Obviously John's Gospel makes no express connection between abundant life and the full actualization of anyone's sexuality. But "abundant life," precisely because of its nonspecificity, is all-encompassing. It can exclude no aspect of human life. And since God wills abundant life for all of God's creation, God's own, on what grounds could we deny that God wills abundant bodily (sexual) life for gays and lesbians as well as for heterosexuals?

Gagnon's appeal to the complementarity of the male and female sex organs, especially the anatomical aspect, may seem inescapably self-evident to us, and this has admirably served the majority of men and women for many millennia; but the self-evident does not cover all the complexities of human interaction. There are subtle dimensions to human and divine-human connections that lie beneath and defy what seems to be palpably obvious. This is well attested in the New Testament, and I give a few examples. Doling out your property or giving up your body is not necessarily proof of love (1 Cor 13:3). God has chosen what is foolish, weak, low, and despised in the world—to the shame of those who are something (1 Cor 1:26-29). God has made the stone that the builders rejected the cornerstone—to the amazement of those who saw it (Mark 12:10-11). Wolves can look like sheep (Matt 7:15). It is not always easy to tell the difference between wheat and weeds (Matt 13:29), for only God can read the heart (Matt 6:4, 6, 18). My point here, of course, is not that any of these texts makes a direct or nonanalogous reference to homosexual practice but that all of them address a critical challenge to Gagnon's frequent appeal to the authority of the self-evident in its palpability.

Should, then, the prohibitions against violating the complementarity of the male and female sex organs always and without exception take precedence over the intention of God that every human creature should be able to express in the fullest way the *only life* to which he or she has been *destined*? For some people homosexual orientation is an inalienable destiny. And from the standpoint of John's Gospel, *all* human beings are God's creatures, God's own created through the Word (1:2-3, 11), for whom God wants abundant life, an aspect of which is bodily (sexual) life. Should then homosexual orientation not be considered a different sexual order of creation, the actualization of which in practice would be natural?

There is more to personal relationships than meets the eye—
there is the puzzling, the unexpected, the ironic. So can we be so
sure that there are not elements in the homosexual orientation
that make homosexual practice natural, despite the absence of
the complementarity of the female and male sex organs? Gagnon
states that there is "no way to demonstrate that homosexual
intercourse, in and of itself, is a good thing" (2001a, 452). If that
is true, by the same token there is no way to demonstrate that it
is a bad thing, in and of itself.

Gagnon tacitly acknowledges this in that his final appeal is to
the absolute *rule*. Same-sex intercourse is absolutely forbidden
in all cases (2001a, 450). "Gratifying a desire for same-sex intercourse is always inherently immoral because the biblical prohibitions are against same-sex intercourse *per se*" (462).

5. *Believers are to manifest to their neighbors the love that
they have experienced from God though Christ.* For Paul God
has poured God's love into our hearts through the Spirit (Rom
5:5), and this gift both makes possible and requires that we show
the same kind of love to our neighbors (1 Cor 12:4, 8-11, 31;
13:1-13; Gal 5:22). Love is both attitude or disposition and act (1
Cor 13:1-7; 2 Cor 8:8-12).

To seek or promote the good or advantage or "thing" of the
other person rather than our own advantage is Paul's most concise and pointed definition of love (Rom 15:1-2; 1 Cor 10:24, 33;
13:5; Phil 2:4; 1 Thess 5:15). Would this not have to mean seeking abundant bodily life for the homosexual since homosexual
orientation is the destiny he/she has been given?

Do we have strong reason to believe that partners in a loving,
mutual, homosexual couple are harming each other by homosexual practice, or are they contributing to each other's well-being?
When the church, in its traditional stance, condemns such people, are we seeking their good or are we harming them and seeking to conceal our own internal insecurities from ourselves?

Here I think we have to listen to the voice of experience.

There are people today who understand themselves as Christians and who are practicing homosexuals who see no incompatibility and feel no tension between these two aspects of their lives (Bird 2000, 143). Listen to these words of Dale Martin, a gay Christian who also happens to be a distinguished New Testament scholar.

> Any interpretation of scripture that hurts people, oppresses people, or destroys people cannot be the right interpretation, no matter how traditional, historical, or exegetically respectable. There can be no debate about the fact that the church's stand on homosexuality has caused oppression, loneliness, self-hatred, violence, sickness, and suicide for millions of people. If the church wishes to continue with its traditional interpretation it must demonstrate, not just claim, that it is more loving to condemn homosexuality than to affirm homosexuals. Can the church show that same-sex loving relationships damage those involved in them? Can the church give compelling reasons to believe that it really would be better for all lesbian and gay Christians to live alone, without the joy of intimate touch, without hearing a lover's voice when they go to sleep or awake? Is it really better for lesbian and gay teenagers to despise themselves and endlessly pray that their very personalities be reconstructed so that they may experience romance like their straight friends? Is it really more loving for the church to continue its worship of "heterosexual fulfillment" (a "nonbiblical" concept, by the way) while consigning thousands of its members to a life of either celibacy or endless psychological manipulations that masquerade as "healing"?
>
> The burden of proof in the last twenty years has shifted. There are too many of us who are not sick, or inverted, or perverted, or even, "effeminate," but who just have a knack for falling in love with people of our own sex. When we have been damaged, it has not been due to our homosexuality but to your and our denial of it. The burden of proof now is not on us, to show that we are not sick, but rather on those who insist that we would be better off going back into the closet. What will "build the double love of God and of our neighbor?" (1996, 130–31)

6. *Biblical revelation is not static but opens into a future of new implications.* I have argued that from the larger context of Scripture and from the contemporary context of science and human experience a case can be made that responsible homosexual practice is morally and theologically justified in Christian terms. Kathryn Greene-McCreight has suggested that there are two types of nontraditional or "revisionist," as she puts it, positions. (1) Some revisionists simply say that the New Testament had in mind abusive pederastic relationships between an adult male and a boy, and thus its condemnation does not apply to consensual, loving, adult relationships. (2) But other revisionists argue that they have a revelation or knowledge that is superior to the New Testament. Against this she argues that as Christians we today stand in a position that is beyond that of Old Testament figures but is not beyond that of the earliest Christians. These revisionists claim to have a revelation that supersedes the New Testament. The New Testament said "no" to homosexual practice, but the revisionists say "yes." This "yes" could be valid only if Jesus had returned and given it (Greene-McCreight 2000, 251, 256–57). Greene-McCreight implies that those who claim a new revelation, or a more advanced eschatological location, are arrogant.

I believe that those who belong to her first revisionist position are in part right. But since I have sought a positive biblical basis for legitimating responsible homosexual practice, I suppose my argument belongs primarily to her second category. I have tried to show that if we look at a number of biblical themes in the light of contemporary knowledge and experience, we can justifiably override the unconditional biblical condemnations of homosexual practice. I can think of two arguments in support of my claim of a new "revelation."

1. In the Bible itself the revelation of God's Word occurs when some person or community within Israel or the church reinterprets past tradition in order to give it new meaning in the present. Revelation occurs as the reinterpretation of tradition. This is

how, for example, the Gospels got written. If the revelation of God is not to remain fixed in the past, the reinterpretive process that produced the Bible must continue in the life of the Christian community. That is what I have been trying to do.

2. If claiming a new position that supersedes the few explicit biblical texts that forbid homosexual practice is arrogant, it is no more than an effort to appropriate what Scripture promises in the Gospel of John. The Jesus of John's Gospel tells his disciples that after he is gone both the Father and he will send the Spirit to remind them of all that he has taught them (14:26; 15:26). More than that, he has many things to say to them that they are not able to bear now. However, when the Spirit comes, he will lead the disciples into all the truth, into implications of Jesus' redemptive mission and message that have not yet come to explicit expression—because they are not yet ready to bear or receive these things (16:12-13).

Again, there is no explicit reference to homosexuality. But "all the truth" is as encompassing as "abundant life." Nothing can be excluded. So why should not a new posture toward homosexuality be understood as a hitherto unrecognized and unacknowledged aspect of all the truth that comes in Jesus, a truth that illuminates an aspect of human existence hitherto constricted by both church and society? Were the church to take an accepting posture toward the moral justifiability of sexual practice in consensual, loving, faithful, homosexual relationships, that would seem to gay and lesbian Christians like the dawning of the Age to Come, the qualitatively new future becoming a reality in the present.

The BIBLE and
HOMOSEXUAL PRACTICE:
KEY ISSUES

ROBERT A. J. GAGNON

The greatest crisis facing the church today is the dispute about homosexual practice. No other issue has so consumed mainline denominations for the past thirty years or holds a greater potential for splitting these denominations.

The reasons are plain. First, owing to Scripture's intense opposition, the debate about same-sex intercourse acutely raises the question of Scripture's place in the life of the church. Second, the homosexuality issue involves the lives of our loved ones in significant ways. Some people do not want church and society to promote, and coerce our children to accept, an unnatural behavior that jeopardizes the standing of its practitioners before God and substantially increases the risk of health and relational problems. Others want to end what they view as a cultural oppression of "gays" and lesbians.

The push for endorsement of homosexual practice represents the key assault today on one of the church's flanks, human sexuality (N1).* A case can be made that, if and when the flank is

* For notes (N) to this section, see www.robgagnon.net.

turned, the results for church and society will be devastating, for these reasons:

1. A radical devaluation of the place of Scripture in the life of the church.
2. A radical devaluation of Scripture's moral imperative—of the place of holiness, obedience, and repentance.
3. Ecclesiastical and civil marginalization, persecution, and even prosecution of those opposed to homosexual practice as the moral equivalent of racists.
4. Coercive indoctrination of our youth into patterns of sexual behavior and belief that the united witness of Scripture deems immoral.
5. An increased incidence of homosexuality and bisexuality in the population, leading to an increase in associated health and relational problems (Gagnon 2001a, 395–429, 452–60, 471–89).
6. *If Scripture is to be trusted,* a heightened risk of loss of salvation for those who actively engage in homosexual behavior.

The push for celebrating homosexual behavior by the pro-homosex lobby is, and will continue to be, the prime catalyst for a sea change in the church's sexual ethics. No other form of behavior so opposed in Scripture is being trumpeted in the church as a positive good (N2). Love mandates that the church resist approval of homosexual behavior while reaching out in humility and gentleness to those afflicted by homoerotic desires.

ON DETERMINING WHAT MATTERS IN SCRIPTURE

When I come to Scripture, I use historical-critical methodology, see development and significant tensions in the canon, take account of metaphors and tradition history, and recognize the necessity of interpreting texts anew. However, in keeping with the historic stance of the church, I also believe that Scripture is the primary authority for faith and practice. If that primacy counts for anything, it must count for core values. Core values are values that are held

1. pervasively throughout Scripture (at least implicitly),
2. absolutely (without exceptions), and . . .
3. strongly (as a matter of significance).

This applies all the more to instances in which:

4. such values emerged in opposition to contrary cultural trends and . . .
5. have prevailed in the church for two millennia.

Such a value is the biblical limitation of sex to intercourse between male and female, with its attendant opposition to all same-sex intercourse.

If the authority of Scripture means anything, those who seek to overturn its core values must meet an extraordinary burden of proof. The evidence must be so strong and unambiguous that it not only makes the witness of Scripture pale by comparison but also directly refutes the reasons for the Bible's position. For example, it would not be enough to prove that (1) the only models for homosexual behavior in antiquity were exploitative, or (2) modern science has demonstrated that homosexuality is congenital and fixed. One would also have to prove that the Bible condemned homosexual practice (3) primarily on the grounds that it was exploitative (e.g., because it abused boys), or (4) on the grounds that all participants in homosexual behavior experienced desires for the opposite sex. As we shall see, none of these points can be substantiated (N3).

THE PROPER USE OF ANALOGIES

Yet are there not instances in which the church has deviated from Scripture's stance? The analogies usually cited are one ancient and several modern ones: (1) the first-century church's inclusion of Gentiles apart from full observance of the Mosaic law; and (2) slavery, women's roles, and divorce. I will show not only that these are poor analogies but also that a far better analogy has been neglected.

The Ancient Analogy: Gentile Inclusion

The argument from Gentile inclusion is that, just as the early church changed its mind about circumcision when it saw the Spirit's work in uncircumcised Gentiles, so too the church today should change its views on homosexual practice as a result of the Spirit's work in the lives of homosexual believers. The main problem with the analogy is that it involves a series of category confusions:

The inclusion of Gentiles involves . . .	The acceptance of homosexual practice involves . . .
• A self-definition based on an immutable objective condition that is 100 percent heritable (ancestry)	• A self-definition based on mutable subjective desire that is not directly heritable (homosexual orientation)
• A self-definition only incidentally linked to sinful behavior	• A self-definition directly linked to sinful behavior
• The noncommission of a positive ritual act (circumcision)	• The commission of negative moral behavior (same-sex intercourse)
• Welcoming people	• Affirming behaviors
• An action that has some Old Testament precedent	• An action that has no Old Testament precedent
• An act with uniform New Testament approval	• An act with no New Testament approval

The differences between the two situations are too great to justify a strong analogy (N4). On the first point: While ethnicity is a condition given at birth, homosexuality is a condition whose incidence society can affect, as cross-cultural studies indicate (Gagnon 2001a, 413–18). On the second point: While first-century Jews could speak of righteous, "God-fearing," uncircumcised Gentiles, the concept of a righteous participant in same-sex intercourse would have been an oxymoron. On the fourth point: The early church learned to accept uncircumcised Gentiles into the faith, but without accepting the sexual behaviors that Scripture deemed immoral (Acts 15; 1 Thess 4:1-8; N5).

Furthermore, if the analogy is applied in such a loose manner, many types of sexual immorality could be justified, so long as: (1) one demonstrates the presence of the Spirit in other areas of one's life; and (2) it cannot be proved that the behavior harms every participant under all circumstances and in scientifically measurable ways. These standards are naïve and unworkable. A person who solicits prostitutes is capable of giving to the poor; and not every instance of plural marriage, incest, promiscuity, commercial sex, pederasty, and bestiality produces measurable distress and maladaptiveness. The church must attend to three other considerations: (1) the degree to which Scripture categorically rejects a given behavior, in contradistinction to the broader culture (N6); (2) indications from nature and reason such as the necessity of avoiding too much structural similarity and dissimilarity; and (3) a statistically verifiable association between a behavior and an increased risk of negative ancillary effects.

The Modern Analogies

1. SLAVERY

Slavery is a very poor analogue (Gagnon 2001a, 443–48).

a. *No mandate.* There is no scriptural mandate to enslave others, nor does one incur a penalty for releasing slaves. Selling oneself into slavery was seen as a last-ditch measure to avoid starvation—at best a necessary evil in a state with limited welfare resources (Lev 25:39). There *is*, however, a scriptural mandate to limit sexual unions to heterosexual ones, with a severe penalty (in this life or the next) imposed on violators.

b. *Not pre-Fall.* Unlike the opposite-sex prerequisite, Scripture does not ground slavery in pre-Fall, that is, "natural" structures. Even if one were to discount this as a dehistoricizing argument, based on myth, the creation stories would still tell us that the biblical writers viewed heterosexual unions, unlike slavery, as normative and transcultural.

c. *The Bible's trajectory of critique.* We can discern a trajectory within the Bible that critiques slavery. Central in Israelite memory was the remembrance of God's liberation from slavery in Egypt (e.g., Exod 22:21; 23:9; Lev 25:42, 55; Deut 15:15). Christian memory adds the paradigmatic event of Christ's redemption of believers from slavery to sin and people (e.g., 1 Cor 6:20; 7:23). Israelite law put various restrictions on enslaving fellow Israelites—even insisting that Israelites not be treated as slaves (N7)—while Paul regarded liberation from slavery as a penultimate good (1 Cor 7:21-23; Phlm 16). While Scripture shows unease with the institution of slavery, the only discomfort it shows toward same-sex intercourse is with the commission of the act, not with its proscription.

d. *The Bible's countercultural witness.* Although the contemporary church's stance on slavery has moved beyond the Bible, the biblical stance was already liberating in relation to the cultures out of which it emerged. The Bible's stance on same-sex intercourse moved in the opposite direction, against any accommodation.

Simply put, Scripture nowhere expresses a vested interest in preserving slavery, whereas Scripture does express a vested interest in requiring a male-female dynamic in sexual relationships (N8).

2. WOMEN IN MINISTRY

The acceptance of women in ministry is also a bad analogy.

a. *Category confusions.* Being a woman is not a mutable condition like the existence of homosexual passions (N9). In Scripture's view, too, being a woman is not a condition directly linked to sinful behavior, as is homoerotic desire.

b. *Subordination post-fall.* While not void of all patriarchal elements, the creation story in Genesis 2–3 traces a husband's rule to the fall, thus a result of sin (3:16).

c. *A positive trajectory in the Bible.* Although the contemporary church has gone further in ordaining women pastors, there are a number of positive precedents in Scripture for putting women in leadership roles (N10). There are no precedents for endorsing homosexual behavior in the Bible.

d. *Meaning of Galatians 3:28.* The Pauline baptismal formula "there is no 'male and female'" affirms the equality of men and women in the new creation. However, Paul certainly did not intend it as grounds for eradicating gender differentiation and affirming every kind of sexual attraction. Nor can it be made to say such without validating a host of aberrant sexual activities (N11).

e. *Countercultural witness.* As with the antislavery impulse in Scripture, the Bible's view of women was reasonably affirming in relation to its cultural world. But the Bible's view of same-sex intercourse stood out as uncompromising (N12).

3. DIVORCE AND REMARRIAGE

The analogy from divorce and remarriage falls short as well (Gagnon 2002, 110–22).

a. *A limited canonical diversity.* The canon of Scripture manifests a limited diversity of opinion on divorce, unlike its uniformly strong rejection of same-sex intercourse. The Old Testament position on divorce is mixed (N13). Jesus did away with the tension by coming down solidly against divorce, thereby removing the concession to male "hardness of heart." Both Matthew and

Paul interpreted Jesus' position as allowing for narrowly defined exceptions: adultery, assumed to be a breach of the marriage bond by definition (5:32; 19:9), or when an unbelieving spouse insists on leaving (1 Cor 7:10-16; N14). The dissolution of a marriage bond in favor of a new one, while serious, is a lesser offense than entering into an unnatural union (N15).

b. *Working to end the cycle.* Most importantly, neither Scripture nor the church celebrates divorce as part of the glorious diversity of the body of Christ. Divorce and same-sex intercourse have in common the fact that both are forgivable sins for those who repent. The church works to end a cycle of divorce and remarriage, just as it ought to work toward the goal of ending a cycle of same-sex intercourse. The *serial, unrepentant* character of much homosexual behavior sets it apart from the divorce issue.

c. *Passive vs. active, involuntary vs. voluntary.* Divorce can occur more or less against one spouse's will. For all the talk about involuntary homoerotic impulses, consensual same-sex intercourse is ultimately a voluntary act. The perpetrator *versus* victim distinction sometimes applies to divorce but never to consenting homoerotic activity, thus injecting a degree of excusableness into the former not germane to the latter.

d. *On consistency.* There is no virtue to being more consistently disobedient to Jesus' teaching (N16). A renewed vision of the utter gravity of the marriage vow is preferable to adopting a standard of anything-consensual-goes. However, even if mainline churches just maintained current standards on divorce and remarriage, it would still be a far cry from the radical departure from Scripture that accepting same-sex intercourse would require. Mainline denominations take a dim view of candidates for ordination who have had a string of divorces. Why, then, should they look the other way when a candidate not only has engaged in same-sex intercourse in the past but also plans to continue such practice in the future?

THE BEST ANALOGY: INCEST

The best analogies are those that most closely match the distinctive elements of the Bible's opposition to same-sex intercourse: consensual sexual behaviors that are pervasively, absolutely, and severely proscribed in both Testaments of Scripture, at least implicitly. What we are left with are forms of sexual behavior that the church continues to proscribe: adultery, prostitution, incest, and bestiality.

Scripture's stance on incest is a particularly good analogy. Both incestuous relationships and homosexual relationships were/are:

1. *Regarded by authors of Scripture with similar revulsion as extreme instances of sexual immorality.* In fact, same-sex intercourse was considered more serious than even incest and adultery, exceeded only by bestiality (N17).

2. *Capable of being conducted in the context of adult, consensual, long-term monogamous relationships.* Needless to say, the immoral quality of sex between a parent and grown child or between two adult siblings is not measurably improved by its being long-term and monogamous.

3. *Wrong partly on the assumption that they involve two people too much alike.* The problem with same-sex intercourse is that it involves two noncomplementary sexual sames or likes. Similarly, incest is sex between familial sames or likes. Incest is wrong because it is sex with the "flesh of one's own flesh" (Lev 18:6). A "one-flesh" union—that is, the establishment of kinship across bloodlines through sexual intercourse—cannot be created between two people who are already of the same "flesh," i.e., close blood relations. Scripture avoids the twin extremes of too much structural identity between sex partners (same-sex intercourse, incest) and too little (bestiality, sex with prepubescent children; N18).

4. *Wrong partly because of the disproportionately high incidence of scientifically measurable, ancillary problems.* One cannot prove that every occurrence of incest produces measurable

harm to all participants. Yet one can demonstrate a disproportionately high rate of associated problems, including higher rates of procreative abnormalities and intergenerational sex. Same-sex intercourse has its own set of ancillary problems: higher rates of sexually transmitted disease, mental health issues, multiple sex partners, short-term relationships, intergenerational sex, problematic sexual practices, and gender identity disorders (Gagnon 2001a, 452–60, 471–83).

No analogy is perfect; but the analogy of incest is clearly superior to the usual analogies of slavery, women's roles, and divorce.

True, incest is not normally a matter of exclusive sexual orientation. Yet three points mitigate this distinction:

1. The exclusivity and intractability of a sexual orientation are not grounds for assessing it as morally good. For example, an exclusive or predominant sexual attraction to children does not improve the moral quality of pedophilic acts (N19).

2. In a functional sense, persons with repressed incestuous desires may find themselves in the same position as persons with repressed homoerotic desires: unable to enter a committed sexual relationship with the person they love. Moreover, the vast majority of self-identified homosexuals experience some heterosexual arousal at some point in life (Gagnon 2001a, 418–20).

3. Cross-culturally speaking, most people develop an early instinctive aversion to incest (N20). Some do not. There may be a combination of biological and environmental factors behind the development of incestuous desires. After all, who would choose to have incestuous desires?

One can show the weakness of arguments for homosexual behavior by making a comparison with incest. Who would argue that:

- A person cannot be held morally accountable for acting on innate incestuous passions?
- To maintain an absolute and strong stance against incest is to forsake grace for law and love for intolerance?

- The Bible's proscriptions of incest should be treated as out-dated purity rules?
- The Levitical imposition of the death penalty on incest is rea-son enough to disregard the proscription?
- Since Jesus said nothing explicit about incest he did not think incest was a major offense?
- If a parent and adult child, or two adult siblings, love one another, it is none of the church's business?
- Intense opposition to incest makes one an "incestphobe"?

Yet similar misplaced arguments are employed to validate homo-sexual practice.

Love and Grace from the Perspective of Jesus and Paul

The central lens through which Scripture must be read is the good news regarding the grace and love of God as manifested in Christ's atoning death and the Spirit's liberating power. Too often this message has been severed in an unbiblical way from concepts of holiness, transformation, and obedience to God's commands.

Jesus on the Double Love Commandment

It is common for many to cite Jesus' appeal to the double love commandment (Mark 12:30-31)—love of God (Deut 6:5) and love of neighbor (Lev 19:18)—as a screen to eliminate scriptural commands that conflict with modern-day notions of tolerance. Difficulties arise with this approach:

1. *It falsely equates love with tolerance of behaviors.* Advocates of this approach often start with a definition of love to which Jesus never subscribed. If by *love* Jesus meant a nonjudgmental accep-

tance of various lifestyles, especially sexual lifestyles, then Jesus' own stance against divorce/remarriage and adultery of the heart was unloving (Matt 5:27-32). Jesus took an already narrow understanding of human sexuality in the Hebrew Scriptures and narrowed it further (N21).

2. *It suppresses the first great commandment.* This approach usually collapses "the great and first commandment" (Matt 22:38), love of God, into the second, love of neighbor, and then defines the latter to embrace behavior that Scripture categorically rejects. This is precisely what Jesus did not do. Persons who violate the commands of God cannot be said to love God whose will they reject, nor the persons made in God's image whom they involve in their corruption.

3. *It overlooks the intertextual echo to Lev 19:17.* Jesus' appeal to Lev 19:18, "you shall love your neighbor as yourself"— a command from the much-maligned Holiness Code (Leviticus 17–26)—reverberates with the echo of Lev 19:17:

> You shall not hate your brother in your heart. *You shall firmly reprove your fellow-countryman and so not incur guilt because of him.* You shall not take revenge and you shall not hold a grudge against any of your people. (italics added)

Love never takes personally a wrong committed. Yet, love often entails reproving another in order to reclaim that person for God's kingdom. If a child is about to touch a hot stove it is not loving to withhold warnings.

4. *It falsely sees an antithesis between outreach to sinners and intensified ethics.* As Jesus' relationship with tax collectors illustrates, true love combines a radical outreach to sinners with an intensification of God's ethical demand. On the one hand, Jesus spoke out against the love of money and sided with the poor. On the other hand, he fraternized with tax collectors who profited from oppressing the poor financially. The Pharisees were unable to get their theological imaginations around these two poles.

They assumed that Jesus' fraternization with sinners meant that
Jesus was cutting ethical corners and they were unhappy with
that. We assume the same thing but are happy with it. Either way
there is a misunderstanding. Jesus calls upon his family, those
who actually *do* the will of God (Mark 3:34-35), to reach out to
sinners without softening by one iota the ethical imperatives of
the kingdom of God (Matt 5:17-20; Luke 16:16-17).

5. *It does not cohere with the theme of judgment in Jesus' teaching.* The stereotype of a Jesus who set love over commandments
and eschewed all judgment simply does not square with the evidence of the Gospels. Even apart from special material in Matthew's Gospel, judgment sayings abound in over one quarter of the
sayings of Jesus in Mark, Q, and special Luke. To claim that talk of
judgment is inherently "unworthy of the highest forms of Christian faith" or "a cruel abuse of religious power" (so Wink 2002b, 44
and 2000a, 34) is to enter the theater of the absurd (N22).

To the church's shame we have taken the central theme of
love and mercy in Jesus' ministry and contorted it to demean
calls for holiness as legalistic. Legalism occurs when the church
uses the commands of God as an excuse for not making every
effort to reclaim the lost for God's kingdom; or when believers
forget the debt that God has forgiven them and fail to extend forgiveness repeatedly to serial backsliders who repent (Luke 17:3-
4; Matt 18:21-22). However, the church is not legalistic when it
recognizes the importance of a transformed life, transformed in
sexual matters, too; nor when it warns of the risk of God's judgment as part of a larger appeal to hope.

One of the best attested set of sayings in the Jesus tradition
puts the point clearly: all who want to follow Jesus must take up
their cross, deny themselves, and lose their lives for Jesus' sake;
otherwise, they will forfeit salvation (Mark 8:34-37; Matt 10:39 //
Luke 17:33; Matt 10:38 // Luke 14:27 // *Gos. Thom.* 55.20; John
12:25). Along the same lines: if one's hand, foot, or eye threatens

to be one's downfall, one should cut it off; for it is better to do that than to have one's whole person thrown into hell (Matt 5:29-30; Mark 9:43-48).

Paul on Law and Grace

A similar distortion comes from truncated notions of the "law/gospel" dichotomy in Paul's letters. Paul declared the Mosaic law to be abrogated since Christ's death and resurrection. No one can be justified, or merit salvation, on the basis of doing "the works of the (Mosaic) law" (N23). Yet, consider the following:

1. *Continuity in God's will.* Paul recognized continuity, especially in sexual ethics, between God's will reflected in the Mosaic law and God's will reflected in the Spirit's leading. This is not surprising. The Giver of the Spirit was the same God as the Giver of the law. Indeed, the Spirit was the law now written on our hearts, no mere external script but an internal regulating power (Jer 31:33-34; Rom 2:29; 7:6).

2. *"Under grace" as the empowerment for doing right.* In the center of Romans 1–11 (6:1—8:17) Paul asks whether believers "should sin since we are not under law but under grace" (6:15). Paul's answer is emphatic: "May it not happen!" If being "under the law" meant being under sin's rule, then being "under grace" must mean liberation from a sin-controlled life (6:16-23; 7:5-6; N24). Jesus' death cleanses the believer of sin, which makes possible the Spirit's indwelling and influence that, in turn, creates a new humanity outside the law's jurisdiction (6:1-14; 8:1-17; 1 Cor 6:12-20; Gal 2:20; 5:13-26).

3. *Freedom from the law only for those led by the Spirit.* Paul asserts that the middle term between freedom from the law and eternal life is "having fruit for holiness" (Rom 6:19-23). The person who confesses Christ as Lord but lives as if sin is lord is in fact a slave of sin and will be recompensed by sin with death. As

Martin Luther put it (commenting on Rom 6:19): "He who serves uncleanness, that is, dissipation and carnal uncleanness, is already becoming more and more unrighteous, for sin now rules over him, and he has lost faith and has become an unbeliever" (N25). Hence, "if you are *led* by the Spirit"—and only so—"you are not subject to the law" (Gal 5:18).

4. No sin transfer without self transfer. The Apostle also maintains that "there is now no condemnation," but only "for those in Christ Jesus," "who walk not according to the flesh but according to the Spirit" and thereby fulfill "the just requirement of the law" (8:1, 4). There is no living in Christ without dying to self (Rom 6:1-14; 7:4-6; 8:1-17; Gal 2:19-20; 5:24-25); no "new creation" without the old passing away (2 Cor 5:15-21); and no citizenship in heaven apart from being conformed to Christ's death and living out of heaven's power, the Spirit (Phil 3:10-11, 20; N26). Paul's ultimate answer to the question in Rom 6:15 is given in 8:12-14: "If you live according to the flesh, you are going to die; but if by the Spirit you put to death the deeds of the body, you will live. For as many as are being *led* by the Spirit, these are the children of God." A confession of faith, unaccompanied by the transformed life, is a sham.

5. Faith as holistic life reorientation. Faith for Paul was not a take-the-money-and-run approach to God's offer of salvation but rather a trust that repeatedly says "Yes" to God and "No" to self. Faith means dying to self and living for God (Gal 2:19-20; N27).

6. Living in the law of the Spirit. Accordingly, Paul can refer to "the law of the Spirit of life in Christ Jesus" freeing us "from the law of sin and death" (Rom 8:2; N28). The abrogation of the law of Moses does not leave believers "lawless." To the contrary: we are subject to the new regulating power of the Spirit. To the Corinthians Paul stated: "I am not without a law toward God but in Christ's law" (1 Cor 9:21). Paul exhorted the Galatian Christians to "fulfill the law of Christ" (Gal 6:2). Paul did not expect perfection, but neither did he expect the Christian life to be static. The mentality is not "do it oneself" but instead "do not resist the Spirit." Self-doing only takes hold when one lives life on one's own terms, "according to the flesh" (N29).

7. *The antithesis of grace and "sexual uncleanness."* It is consistent with this broader theological context that Paul regarded serial, unrepentant participation in *porneia* and *akatharsia* as incompatible with the grace of God. *Porneia* means "sexual immorality" (cf. English *pornography*), including incest, male-male intercourse, adultery, solicitation of prostitutes, and fornication (so *porneia* and *pornos*, "sexually immoral person," in 1 Cor 5–7; N30). Paul normally used the word *akatharsia*, "uncleanness, impurity, filthy conduct," as a synonym for *porneia*, denoting "dirty" sexual practices. In Rom 1:24-27 Paul treats same-sex intercourse as the prime example of "sexual uncleanness" (*akatharsia*). Often *porneia* and *akatharsia* appear in combination, sometimes alongside *aselgeia* ("licentiousness," the condition of being without sexual self-restraint), and listed *first* (sometimes second, after idolatry) among behaviors that can get Christians excluded from God's coming kingdom: 1 Thess 4:2-8; Gal 5:19-21 (cf. 6:7-9); 1 Cor 6:9-11; 2 Cor 12:21; Rom 1:24-27; 6:19; cf. Col 3:5-10; Eph 4:17-19; 5:3-6; 1 Tim 1:9-11 (N31). Paul's point in these passages could not be clearer: sex matters. He repeatedly warns his readers to "stop deceiving yourselves" into thinking that immoral believers will escape wrath. In Rom 6:19 Paul is emphatic about the necessity of moral transformation: "just as you [once] presented your [bodily] members as slaves to sexual uncleanness [*akatharsia*, paralleling 'slaves of sin' in 6:16-23] . . . for lawlessness, so now present your members as slaves to righteousness for holiness." The "end" or outcome of such moral transformation is "eternal life"; but of the untransformed life the opposite, "death," everlasting separation from the life of God (6:20-23; cf. 7:5-6; 8:12-14). Paul emphasized to the Corinthian believers what grace and redemption are for: "Flee *porneia*. . . . Or don't you know that your body is a temple

of the Holy Spirit . . . and you are not your own? For you were bought with a price. *So glorify God in your body"* (1 Cor 6:18-20).

Anyone who contends on the basis of a Pauline (or Lutheran) law/gospel distinction that attention to commandments, especially as regards sexual behavior, is a legalism that subverts the gospel of grace has not understood Paul (or Luther). Paul insisted that what matters is "keeping the commandments of God" (1 Cor 7:19) and did so within a broader discussion of sexual purity (1 Corinthians 5–7). What we do with our bodies sexually is an essential part of what it means to "present [our] bodies as a living sacrifice, holy, pleasing to God" (Rom 12:1).

THE PERVASIVE STANCE AGAINST HOMOSEXUAL PRACTICE IN THE OLD TESTAMENT

Most pro-homosex scholars argue that the Old Testament speaks to the issue of homosexual practice on only four occasions: the twin stories of Sodom (Gen 19:1-9) and the Levite at Gibeah (Judg 19:22-25) and the two Levitical proscriptions (Lev 18:22; 20:13). They then discount each set, claiming that the two narratives refer only to homosexual gang rape, while the two Levitical proscriptions are antiquated purity rules. However, the Old Testament has a web of additional interconnecting texts that establish an indictment of same-sex intercourse per se and provide a reasonable basis for rejecting such behavior (Gagnon 2001a, 43–110, 146–57).

The Story of Ham's Act against Noah

There are strong grounds for understanding Ham's sin of "seeing the nakedness of his father" Noah as a reference to incestuous, homosexual rape (Gen 9:20-27; cf. Lev 20:17; N32). To be sure, one might still claim that, like the stories of Sodom and Gibeah, the story of Ham indicts only coercive forms of male-male intercourse. Yet matters are not quite so simple, for two reasons.

1. Few would argue that only coercive forms of incest are implicitly denounced in the story. It seems highly unlikely, then, that only coercive acts of male-male intercourse are in view. This is a "kitchen sink" story whose purpose is to show how truly bad the ancestor of the Canaanites was by multiplying heinous offenses: not just rape but also a case of incest and of male-male intercourse.

2. Bringing the Ham story into the homosex debate establishes an ideological connection with Leviticus 18, since both texts attribute God's judgment of the Canaanites to their egregious sexual practices. The sexual sins indicted in Leviticus 18—among which incest and male-male intercourse are featured—do not refer exclusively to coercive acts.

Consequently, it is likely that the narrator of Gen 9:20-27 (the "Yahwist," J) viewed incest and same-sex intercourse per se as compounding factors in the heinous quality of Ham's aggression. This would, in turn, increase the likelihood that the Yahwist understood his other story of homosexual rape, the Sodom narrative, in the same light.

Subsequent Interpretation of the Sodom Narrative: Ezekiel, Jude, and 2 Peter

Ezekiel states that Sodom "did not take hold of the poor and the needy. And they grew haughty and committed an abomination (to'evah) before me" (16:49-50). Pro-homosex scholars usually interpret "abomination" to refer to economic injustice. This is not a likely interpretation, for three reasons:

1. In a list of vices in 18:10-13, Ezekiel distinguishes "commits an abomination" (singular) from both "oppresses the poor and the needy" and the concluding summary statement, "committed all these abominations" (plural).

2. Ezekiel shows strong links with the Holiness Code (Leviticus 17–26), especially in Ezekiel 18. It is not mere coincidence that Leviticus 18 likewise specifically tags male-male intercourse as an "abomination" (singular; 18:22), even as it summarizes all the offenses as "abominations" (plural; 18:24-30).

3. Given that the two other singular uses of "abomination" in Ezekiel refer to sexual sins (22:11; 33:26), it is likely that Ezekiel intends "abomination" in 16:50 and 18:12 as a metonym or substitute for male-male intercourse (N33).

This means that Ezekiel read the Sodom story in the light of the Levitical prohibitions of male-male intercourse; that is, he interpreted male-male intercourse per se as an abomination. As with the Yahwist's story of Ham, Ezekiel's reading creates an early ideological nexus between the Sodom story and Leviticus 18.

Jude 7 alludes to the sin of Sodom and Gomorrah as "in a manner similar to these (the angels who copulated with women), having committed sexual immorality (*ekporneusasai*) and gone after other flesh." The meaning of the text is probably that, in their lust for sexual intercourse with other males, the men of Sodom *inadvertently* put themselves in the sacrilegious position of pursuing sexual intercourse with angels (the "other flesh"). To read the offense as a reference to a desire to have sex with angels is unlikely, for three reasons:

1. The history of interpretation of the Sodom episode assumes that the men of Sodom were unaware of the visitors' angelic status and intended to have sex with human males (N34).

2. Jude 8 states that the false believers against whom Jude was writing "likewise also defile (stain, pollute) (the/their) flesh,

reject lordships, and slander the glorious ones" (i.e., angels). The false believers' lust for immoral sexual behavior had put them on a collision course with the angelic guardians of this world order, which subsequently led them to revile angels, not to lust after them (v. 8). In a similar way, the immoral sexual desire of the Sodomites, in this case for male-male intercourse, led them to pursue sex with angels unknowingly.

3. This interpretation of Jude 7 fits best with Second Peter's own interpretation of Jude 7–8, referring as it does to the "sexual licentiousness (*aselgeia*) of conduct of the lawless" at Sodom (2:7) and to those following in their footsteps as "going after (i.e., indulging) (the/their) flesh in (or: with its) defiling desire" (2:7, 10). The "defiling desire" of the Sodomites can only be their desire to "know" Lot's male visitors, whom they did not yet recognize as angels (N35).

Read with other Jewish texts of the period, the authors of Jude and 2 Peter undoubtedly understood a key offense of Sodom to be men desiring to have sex with males (N36).

Light from the Deuteronomistic History

Another strand in the web of interconnected homosexual texts is the series of Deuteronomic and Deuteronomistic references to the *qedeshim* (sg. *qadesh*), "homosexual cult prostitutes" (Deut 23:17-18; 1 Kgs 14:21-24; 15:12-14; 22:46; 2 Kgs 23:7; also Job 36:13-14; Rev 22:15 with 21:8; N37). The labeling of this phenomenon recurring in unfaithful periods of Judah's history as an "abomination" (*to'evah*), coupled with the fact that it was Judah's most profiled form of homosexual behavior, indicates a connection with the Levitical proscriptions. But from which direction? There is little basis for arguing that the broadly worded Levitical proscriptions applied only to the specific case of the *qedeshim* (below). Rather, the absoluteness of the Levitical proscriptions suggests that the authors of Deuteronomy and the Deuteronomistic history also found same-sex intercourse to be offensive per se and not just when it involved idolatry or the exchange of money. Parallel cult functionaries in Mesopotamia, known as the *assinnu*, were disparaged as "men-women" and "dogs" (cf. Deut 23:18) because of their receptive role in male-male intercourse, blurring as they did their own gender identity as males (cf. the prohibition of cross-dressing in Deut 22:5). Since in Mesopotamia this was the *most* acceptable context for playing the passive male homosexual role, the Deuteronomistic stance must have in view "the repugnant associations with male homoerotic activity" (Bird 1997, 75). Moreover, revulsion for the *qedeshim* has nothing to do with rape.

Consequently, the Deuteronomistic historian would have interpreted the attempt at penetrating the Levite at Gibeah in Judg 19:22-25 as an inherently degrading act, regardless of consent. Since the story in Judg 19:22-25 closely parallels the story of Sodom in Gen 19:4-11—indeed, significant verbatim agreement indicates literary dependence—we have another early attestation of how to read the offense of the Sodomites: not just inhospitable rape of strangers but putting the male visitors into the category of female so far as sexual intercourse is concerned. Or, as the Levitical proscriptions put it: men "lying with a male as though lying with a woman."

The Ancient Near Eastern Context

Since there are ancient Near Eastern texts that disparage males who play the role of females in sexual intercourse (Gagnon 2001a, 44–56), it is highly unlikely that either the narrators of the stories of Ham, Sodom, and Gibeah, or their audiences viewed these stories as indicting only coercive acts. Surely ancient Israelite attitudes toward homoerotic activity were not more favorable than those that prevailed in the ancient Near East.

The Contribution of the Creation Stories
in Genesis 1–3

There are also transparent connections between the Yahwist's stories about Ham and Sodom and his account of the creation of woman. In Gen 2:18-24, a binary or sexually undifferentiated human (the *adam*) is split into two sexually differentiated beings. Marriage is treated by the Yahwist as a reunion of two complementary sexual others, a reconstitution of the sexual unity of the original *adam*. One can no more dismiss the story's implicit relevance for proscriptions of same-sex intercourse than one can dismiss its pertinence for attitudes against bestiality (cf. 2:20). The splitting creates not just two humans but two sexually differentiated humans. Two males or two females in sexual union would not equal an originally binary being or sexual whole. A restoration of "one-fleshness" requires a male and female because the missing element is the opposite sex: "therefore a man shall . . . cleave to his woman/wife and the two shall become one flesh" (2:24). Genesis 2:24 advances not just the normal state of affairs but, implicitly, a prescriptive norm, as both Jesus and Paul recognized (Mark 10:7; 1 Cor 6:16). To convey the legitimacy of homoerotic unions a different kind of creation story is needed—the kind of story spun by Aristophanes in Plato's *Symposium* (189c-193d) where an original male-male, female-female, and male-female are split (Gagnon 2001a, 353–54). When one adds to the Yahwist's stories of creation, Ham, and Sodom the fact that all other references to sexual relationships in his work presume a prescriptive heterosexual norm, the only historically responsible conclusion is that the Yahwist opposed same-sex intercourse per se (on Gen 1–3, see Gagnon 2003, IV).

Similarly, it is implausible to suggest that the narrators of Genesis 1 (the Priestly Writers, P) did not understand the implications of their story about the creation of male and female and God's blessing upon their sexual union for ruling out all same-sex

intercourse. Nor can one limit their concern to matters of procreation, given the narrators' special attention to issues of structural congruity or "kinds." Once more, both Jesus and Paul
regarded Gen 1:26-27 as a prescriptive, not just descriptive, heterosexual norm (Mark 10:6; echoed in Rom 1:23-27).

The Implications of the Rest of the Old Testament Canon

In the Bible the whole range of narratives, laws, proverbs, exhor-
tations, metaphors, and poetry, insofar as they have to do with
human sexuality, presume the sole and exclusive legitimacy of
heterosexual unions. There is not a single piece of evidence any-
where in the Old Testament that even hints at a favorable attitude toward any kind of homosexual relationship. The David and
Jonathan narratives are no exception (Gagnon 2001a, 146–54). It
comes as no surprise, then, that the subsequent witness of early
Judaism is one of unremitting opposition to same-sex intercourse—a rigor unmatched by any other culture in the Mediterranean basin (Gagnon 2001a, 159–83).

THE LEVITICAL PROSCRIPTIONS AND THE ISSUE OF PURITY

The two legal texts in the Levitical Holiness Code (N38) pro-
scribing male-male intercourse read:

> With a male you shall not lie as though lying with a woman; it
> is an abomination. (18:22)

> And a man who will lie with a male as though lying with a
> woman, they have committed an abomination, the two of
> them; they shall certainly be put to death; their blood be upon
> them. (20:13)

Though we understand that the Mosaic law has been abrogated in Christ, material therein still has relevance for discerning God's will in a new covenant dispensation (cf. Lev 19:18). There are at least seven good reasons why Lev 18:22 and 20:13 remain relevant to the church today (Gagnon 2001a, 111–46).

Part of a Broader Old Testament Witness

Because they cohere with a picture of strong opposition to homosexual practice in ancient Israel, the Levitical proscriptions of male-male intercourse cannot be characterized as a quirk of the Holiness Code (N39).

Absoluteness Transcending Exploitative Forms

The wording of these proscriptions is unqualified and absolute, which makes it difficult to restrict their relevance only to certain exploitative forms of male-male intercourse.

1. The word "male" (*zakar*) is used, not "homosexual cult prostitute" (*qadesh*), "boy, youth" (*na'ar*), or even "your neighbor" (*re'akah*).

2. Like the other sex rules of ch. 18, 18:22 applies to the Israelite and the resident non-Israelite alike (18:26).

3. Both parties are penalized so, clearly, the prohibition has in view consensual male-male intercourse.

4. The absolute wording precludes any limitation of the proscription to the *qedeshim*, as do two other points: (a) the location of 20:13 amidst other broadly defined illicit sex acts; and (b) the fact that male cult prostitution was the most acceptable form in which receptive male-male intercourse could be practiced in the ancient Near East.

5. The absoluteness of the prohibition is unlike anything else found in the ancient Near East or Greece—contexts that made accommodations depending on active role, consent, age or social

status of the passive partner (alien, slave, foreigner), and/or cultic association (N40).

Grouped with Other Relevant Sex Proscriptions

The prohibitions occur next to other sex acts that we mainly continue to prohibit today: incest, adultery, bestiality, and the not unrelated matter of child sacrifice (N41).

A First-Tier Sexual Offense

Unlike some now defunct elements of the Holiness Code, male-male intercourse receives a very strong and absolute indictment (N42). In Leviticus 20 male-male intercourse appears in the midst of other first-tier sexual offenses punishable by a death sentence: adultery, sex with one's stepmother or with one's daughter-in-law, male-male sex, marriage to mother and daughter at the same time, and human-animal sex (20:10-16; N43). The penalty for male-male intercourse exceeds anything known in the ancient Near East (N44). Today we discard the penalty for each of the offenses in Lev 20:10-16 but not the emphatic prohibition. The penalty still underscores the seriousness of the offense (N45). Although Lev 18:24-30 refers to all the sex offenses in ch. 18 as *to'evoth*—"abominations; things abhorrent, detestable, loathsome, or repugnant"—male-male intercourse is alone specifically tagged with this word (N46). Outside Leviticus the word is nearly always used of acts that are idolatrous, sexually immoral, or socially exploitative—acts that the church still finds offensive (Gagnon 2001a, 117–20).

The Necessity of Sexual Complementarity

The reason why male-male intercourse is wrong is implicit in the proscription itself: "lying with a male as though lying with a woman." Male-male intercourse puts a male in the category of female so far as sexual intercourse is concerned. Because sexual intercourse is about sexual completion it requires complementary sexual others. Anatomy and physiology provide two transparent clues to a *broad* range of discomplementary features in homoerotic unions.

Some scholars pinpoint the nonprocreative dimension as the primary motive behind the Levitical proscriptions (N47). This is tantamount to contending that, if not for procreation problems, sex with one's mother or another man's wife or one's sheep would have been acceptable. At stake are broader category issues: not having sex with too much of an "other" (bestiality) or too much of a "like" (incest, male-male intercourse), and not disrupting the one-flesh bond of a legitimate sexual union (adultery; N48).

Other scholars argue that misogyny (the hatred of women) is at the heart of the Levitical proscriptions: men not wanting to become that inferior creature called woman. The theory is, at best, reductionistic (Gagnon 2001a, 139–42). Certainly it cannot be substantiated from Gen 2:18-24. Here man yearns to become joined again, in one-flesh union, with his other half, his sexual "counterpart" and "helper." The story beautifully illustrates a holistic fittedness to a man-woman union, in terms of anatomy, procreation, sexual stimulation, relational expectations, and other gender differences that we today characterize with the slogan "men are from Mars and women are from Venus." Holiness entails wholeness. Another male cannot supply the missing sexual dimension in a man, not even if the former "does his best" to play the feminine part. At most he can offer only variations of the same masculine stamp (N49). There is nothing wrong with men seeking validation of their sexual identity from other males. Yet when this becomes sexualized, such that one perceives union with a sexual same as self-completion, then something distorted has happened: a denial of the integrity of the sexual self.

Purity Buttressing Morality

The attachment of purity language to the sexual offenses in
Leviticus 18 (vv. 19, 20, 23-30) and their absoluteness are no
arguments for dismissing these laws as "nonrational and pre-
ethical" (*pace* Bird 2000, 150–57).

1. The conjunction of purity and prohibition often buttresses
a moral judgment by focusing on the inherently degrading
character of the act for participants and its destabilizing effects
for the community. Society sends a message to would-be trans-
gressors that self-rationalizations are irrelevant. The sense of
divine wrath, communal outrage, and individual shame con-
veyed by pollution taboos provides psychological support to
civil penalties, banishing from most minds even the thought of
transgression (N50).

2. Pollution taboos play a particularly important role in curb-
ing illicit sexual behavior. Paul's almost exclusive application of
the term *akatharsia*, "uncleanness, impurity," to immoral sex
acts underscores this role. Civil sanctions have only limited
effectiveness in a context where the pleasure is so intense, the
setting so private, and the self-justification so artful. Even today
a number of sexual offenses continue to carry a strong social
stigma. Few bemoan this state of affairs (N51).

3. Any attempt to draw hard distinctions between sin and
impurity is doomed to failure. Indeed, one of the hallmarks of
the Holiness Code is that it incorporates ethics under the rubric
of purity; that is, sin and impurity merge (N52). Hence in the
summary in Lev 18:24-30 it is the "iniquity" or "sin" (*awon*) of
the aforementioned "abominations" (*to'evoth*) that brings about
defilement (v. 25). Ezekiel, who has affinities with the Holiness
Code, combines the language of sin and impurity when criticizing idolatry, economic exploitation, and sexual immorality (e.g.,
chapters 18, 22, 36; N53).

4. It is not true that one moves away from the realm of sin to
the realm of the pre-rational and non-ethical when one dis-

counts the loving disposition of the participants. First, intention and motive are not entirely eliminated from the Levitical proscriptions: a person raped is not penalized. Second, like the Holiness Code, Paul's treatment of same-sex intercourse, incest, adultery, and fornication discounts a loving disposition (1 Corinthians 5–7; Rom 1:24-27; 1 Thess 4:3-8). Yet hardly any scholars nowadays contend that Paul understood these acts as unclean but not sinful (N54). Third, we rightly continue to proscribe many behaviors irrespective of a loving disposition, including sex with one's parent, sibling, a child, two persons at the same time, or an animal.

Appropriation by the New Testament

Lastly, if indeed the Levitical proscriptions of male-male intercourse were nothing more than pre-rational relics of an outmoded purity system, why then did Paul appropriate them for the new covenant dispensation? The compound term *arsenokoitai* in 1 Cor 6:9, "men lying with males," is almost certainly derived from the Septuagint (Greek) translation of Lev 18:22 and 20:13, which employs the words "male" (*arsēn*) and "lying" (*koitē*). Jews and Christians using the term deliberately echoed their law's distinctive proscription of men penetrating other males—the most acceptable form of homoerotic activity in the ancient world. "Pagans" did not use the term. Paul made further allusions to Leviticus 18 and 20 both in the context of 1 Cor 6:9 and in Rom 1:24-27 (N55). In line with Jesus' own special concern for sex ethics, Paul gave critical consideration to which sex laws should be expanded, maintained, or eliminated in the new covenant (N56). Paul understood the difference between defunct purity rules and abiding moral values and placed Lev 18:22 and 20:13 in the latter category (N57).

When Paul stated in Rom 14:14 that he was "convinced in the Lord Jesus that nothing is unclean (*koinon*) in itself," he was referring to the ritual impurity attributed to *objects*—in this case meat. He distinguished between ritual impurity, requiring washing and the passage of time, and moral impurity, requiring repentance. Given the approach that Paul took toward the incestuous man in 1 Corinthians 5, he obviously did not think all adult sexual *behavior* motivated by a loving disposition should be considered morally clean. Neither do we. Consequently, when Paul referred to sexual immorality in general and same-sex intercourse in particular as "uncleanness," he was not reinterpreting Old Testament impurity language as sin. Rather, he was using purity language in line with much of his scriptural heritage (N58).

The Witness of Jesus

Many pro-homosex advocates argue that Jesus' silence about same-sex intercourse indicates, minimally, that Jesus did not have strong convictions about the subject. Or, maximally, that Jesus would have approved of homosexual unions—perhaps even that he did so in the case of the centurion and his slave (Matt 8:5-13; Luke 7:1-10; N59). Actually, though Jesus did not speak directly to the issue, there is significant inferential evidence that he maintained Scripture's strong rejection of homosexual behavior (Gagnon 2001a, 185–228).

The Background of Early Judaism

Jesus' alleged silence has to be set against the backdrop of unequivocal and univocal opposition throughout early Judaism (N60). In such a setting silence means agreement with the only viewpoint that existed in the public discourse of early Judaism, especially since Jesus was not shy about disagreeing with the conventions of his day. Had he wanted his disciples to take a different viewpoint he would have had to say so.

Jesus' Position on the Mosaic Law

The common notion in the church today that Jesus overturned the Mosaic law is a misrepresentation.

1. Jesus prioritized "the weightier matters of the law" while still urging that lesser matters, such as tithing herbs, not be neglected (Matt 23:23; Luke 11:42). He also amended the law for greater internal consistency. As the six antitheses in Matt 5:21-48 indicate, normally this meant closing the law's loopholes and intensifying its demands. Jesus insisted that "not one tiny letter stroke of the law" shall be dispensed with (Matt 5:17-18; Luke 16:17; N61).

2. A common assumption is that Jesus, already in his earthly ministry, put an end to all laws having to do with food, Sabbath, and purity. Given the sayings cited above, this is probably not the case (see also Mark 1:44). The saying in Mark 7:15-19 about what defiles a person is often cited as proof that Jesus abolished the food laws. It is more likely that Jesus intended a hyperbolic contrast: what counts most is not what goes into a person but what comes out (N62).

3. If Jesus did not abrogate even such things as food laws and meticulous tithing, then it is impossible that he would have overturned a proscription of sexual immorality as serious as that of male-male intercourse. Jesus was a less vigorous critic of the law than Paul (N63). If Paul, along with the rest of the leadership of early Christianity, believed that he was following Jesus in viewing same-sex intercourse as the epitome of Gentile sexual uncleanness, then there is little or no chance that Jesus harbored a secret acceptance of such behavior (N64).

The Myth of a Sexually Tolerant Jesus

Although it is widely believed in liberal circles that Jesus lowered the bar on issues of sexual ethics, the reverse is the case.

1. The three stories of sexual sinners. Jesus reached out to sexual sinners. The key stories are: the sinful woman in Luke 7:36-50; the woman caught in adultery in John 7:53—8:11; and the Samaritan woman at the well in John 4. They no more suggest that Jesus was soft on sexual sin than do the stories about Jesus' fraternization with tax collectors insinuate an accommodation to economic exploitation. The subtext for all three stories is that the sexual lives of the women were turned around by Jesus' unexpected outreach. Indeed, Jesus was motivated by the concern that they would face judgment at the kingdom's coming (N65).

2. Seeking the sexually lost with repentance in view. Jesus did not promote a repentance-less inclusion in God's kingdom. Rather, the distinctive features of his ministry were: (1) an intensive effort to search for the lost; (2) exultation at their joyous return, with full and immediate inclusion; and (3) grace for those who repeatedly "backslide" but repent each time (Luke 17:3-4; Matt 18:21-22). *Being lost* was an image for a gravely sinful pattern of behavior, not for being unjustly marginalized. *Finding* denoted restoration of another to a life of holiness in fellowship with God (N66).

3. The parable of the Good Samaritan. Some pro-homosex scholars misuse this parable (Luke 10:28-35) to advocate support for homosexual practice. The parable is actually about reconceptualizing enemies consigned to death as neighbors to be directed lovingly into the path of life. When one asks the question "Who is my neighbor that I must love?" (cf. Lev 19:18) from the vantage point of one lying half dead by the side of the road, the perspective is significantly different from that of someone who asks the same question from a social location of security and comfort. The parable illustrates the Golden Rule: whatever you want people to do for you, do for them (Matt 7:12; Luke 6:31). Loving the homosexual neighbor does not mean affirming homoerotic behavior. It means discouraging it in the context of a loving outreach (N67).

4. Narrowing further the permissible range of sexual activity. One of the most remarkable things about Jesus' mission was that in the context of an aggressive outreach to the lost he deepened God's demand for sexual purity. Instead of advocating that divorce and remarriage be as easy for women as for men, he declared that "whoever divorces his wife" both "commits adultery" when he marries another and becomes partly responsible for his wife's adultery when she remarries; moreover, that a man who "marries a divorced woman commits adultery" (Matt 5:32; Luke 16:18; Mark 10:11-12; 1 Cor 7:10-11). Jesus was virtually without peer in his radical insistence on limiting the number of lifetime sex partners to one. His saying about adultery of the heart severely constrained not only behavior but also thoughts (Matt 5:27-28). So seriously did he take sexual immorality that he told people that it was better to cut off the offending body part than to have the whole person thrown into hell (Matt 5:29-30; Mark 9:43-48). Most pro-homosex advocates feel certain that Jesus would never have denied a sexual relationship to two exclusive homosexuals in love with one another. In view of Jesus' unprecedented narrowing of the range of legitimate sexual intercourse, it is hard to think of someone for whom the consideration of "sexual starvation" as a basis for violating a biblical sex norm would have had less impact (N68).

Sayings of Jesus Implicitly Forbidding Same-Sex Intercourse

1. Jesus on sex at creation. The key text appears in the context of Jesus' discussion of divorce in Mark 10:1-12. When Jesus cited back-to-back Gen 1:27 (*"male* and *female* he made them"*) and Gen 2:24 (*"For this reason a man* . . . will be joined to his *woman* [wife], and the two will become one flesh"*), he obviously understood with all Jews of his day that an absolute prerequisite was that the two participants be male and female, man and woman (10:6-8; N69). That Jesus focused on two phrases, "God made" and "will be joined"—thereby emphasizing the indissolubility of the one valid sexual union—does not mean that he treated the genders of the participants as nonessential. On the contrary, both the Scriptures that Jesus cited and the audience that he addressed presumed the requisite complementarity of the sexes. Jesus clearly agreed. The creation stories in Genesis 1–2 depict marriage as the remerger of the two sexes split off from the original binary human. Moreover, with his remark "but from the beginning of creation [it was thus]," it is apparent that Jesus saw the creation stories not merely as descriptive but as prescriptive; in short, as normative for human sexual relations (Gagnon 2003, IV, E).

2. *Jesus on sexual immoralities.* Mark states that Jesus interpreted his own saying about what defiles a person to mean: "for it is from . . . the human heart that evil intentions come: sexual immoralities (*porneiai*) . . . adulteries . . . licentiousness (*aselgeia*). . . . All these evil things come from within and defile a person" (Mark 7:21-23). No first-century Jew could have spoken of *porneiai* (sexual immoralities) without having in mind the list of forbidden sexual offenses in Leviticus 18 and 20, particularly incest, adultery, same-sex intercourse, and bestiality. In Mark's understanding, the point is that food, an inanimate object, pertains only to the stomach. Yet some behaviors, especially sexual behaviors, corrupt the whole person (the heart). The desire to engage in them is *inherently* self-defiling. There is no justification for arguing that Jesus instructed his followers to disregard absolute proscriptions and to use instead the disposition of the participants as the new criterion for approval (N70).

3. *Jesus on the Decalogue command against adultery.* Jesus subscribed to the seventh commandment, "You shall not commit adultery." One does not need a saying or story in the Jesus tradition to establish this, though we have one in Mark 10:17-22. It was common in early Judaism to regard the Ten Commandments as containing the broad headings for the laws in the Pentateuch. Philo, for example, treated the sex laws in the Bible, including the proscriptions of male-male intercourse, under the

commandment against adultery (*Special Laws* 3.1-82). Since the seventh commandment aims at the preservation of the man-woman marital bond and none other, any instance of sexual intercourse outside that bond would be precluded as a matter of course. Jesus too would have viewed this commandment as pre-supposing the sole legitimacy of heterosexual marriage (N71).

4. Jesus on Sodom. When Jesus declared that "it will be more tolerable on the Day (of Judgment) for Sodom" than for towns that do not welcome his messengers (Luke 10:10-12; Matt 10:14-15), he was acknowledging Sodom's role in Scripture as the prime example of abuse of visitors. As noted above, ancient interpretations of the story of Sodom and Gomorrah that go beyond passing references show a special revulsion for the ghastly attempt at treating males sexually as females. Jesus prob-ably accepted this common interpretation but then gave it a novel twist: as bad as the actions of the men of Sodom were, fail-ure to welcome Jesus and his emissaries was worse still because "something more than" an angelic visitation was here (Luke 11:29-32; Matt 12:39-41).

5. Jesus on the qedeshim. The saying "Do not give that which is holy to the dogs" in Matt 7:6 may contain an intertextual echo to Deut 23:17-18. The latter refers to the *qadesh*—usually translated "homosexual cult prostitute" but literally "holy man" (N72)—as a "dog" (similarly, Rev 22:15). Jesus' saying would be a logical exten-sion of the command in Deut 23:17-18 not to allow "dogs" to give money received from abominable practices to the holy place: if the temple is too holy to receive the fees from homosexual cult prostitutes, then the message of the kingdom, which was holier still, should not be entrusted to those who mock holiness through their continuance in abominable practices (N73).

Given these implicit rejections, the reason that Jesus did not speak explicitly against same-sex intercourse is obviously the same reason why he did not speak explicitly against incest and bestiality: (1) the position of the Hebrew Bible on such matters was so unequivocal and visceral, and (2) the stance of early Judaism so undivided, with (3) the incidence of concrete violations so rare, that nothing more needed to be said. There was no reason for him to spend time addressing issues that were not points of contention and on which he had no dissenting view. Jesus could turn his attention to sexual issues that were problems in his society: the threat posed by divorce and by sexually errant thoughts to the one valid form of sexual union—that between a man and a woman. Jesus did not loosen the restrictions on sexual freedom; he tightened them, albeit in the context of an aggressive outreach to the lost.

The Witness of Paul

Some pro-homosex apologists give the impression that Paul's strong stance against homosexual practice was an anomaly in the New Testament. They then treat the allegedly unclear references to male-male intercourse in 1 Cor 6:9 and 1 Tim 1:10 in isolation from Paul's clear statement in Rom 1:24-27. Finally, they discount Rom 1:24-27 by using one or more of the following main arguments:

• *The exploitation argument.* Paul was thinking only of exploitative forms of homoerotic behavior—pederasty (love of boys), sex with slaves, prostitution, and/or homoeroticism in the context of idolatrous cults—so we cannot know what Paul would have thought about committed adult relationships (Scroggs, Martin).

• *The orientation argument.* Paul had no concept of a homosexual "orientation"—a relatively fixed and congenitally based disposition—so we cannot know what Paul would have thought about same-sex intercourse between two people exclusively oriented toward the same sex (Nissinen 1998, Wink 1999).

• *The misogyny argument.* Paul was opposed to same-sex intercourse because he feared that homoerotic unions would upset the hierarchical dominance of men over women (Bird, Brooten, Nissinen, Fredrickson, Moore).

The evidence that we have does not support any of these three positions (Gagnon 2001a, 347–95).

Paul's View as the New Testament Norm

Paul's strong opposition to same-sex intercourse is no more an isolated view in the New Testament than his intense rejection of incest (1 Corinthians 5). Historically speaking, it is the *only* view (Gagnon 2001a, 432–41). An isolated view, were it to exist, would be any indication of affirmation for same-sex intercourse. The implicit rejection of same-sex intercourse in the Jesus tradition tells us what Matthew, Mark, and Luke believed. Moreover, the Apostolic Decree referred to by Luke in Acts (15:20, 29; 21:25) was formulated from the laws in Leviticus 17–18, laws binding even on resident aliens. The Decree's requirement that Gentile believers abstain from *porneia* ("sexual immorality") undoubtedly embraced, if only by implication, the Levitical proscription of male-male intercourse in 18:12, in agreement with the "Noahide laws" developing in early Judaism (N74). The references to Sodom in Jude and 2 Peter and to the abominable "dogs" in Revelation confirm a consensus against same-sex intercourse. Every narrative, moral exhortation, and metaphor in the New Testament that has anything to do with human sexuality presumes the sole legitimacy of opposite-sex unions. Paul—at least the Paul of the undisputed Pauline corpus—had the most radical view of the law's abrogation and the most "liberal" social ethics of any New Testament author. If even he opposed same-sex intercourse, it is very unlikely that any New Testament author held a different view. All talk of same-sex intercourse being a minor concern in the New

Testament, based on frequency of its explicit mention, denies the importance of historical context for biblical interpretation (N75).

Romans 1:24-27:
Does Paul Indict All Same-Sex Intercourse?

The literary context of Rom 1:24-27 is Paul's broad indictment of humanity in 1:18—3:20 for sinning against the knowledge of God accessible to them (Gagnon 2001a, 240–53). For Gentiles that knowledge was available in creation/nature (1:19-32); for Jews in Scripture as well (2:1—3:20). As regards the former, humans "suppressed the truth" about God's image-shattering "power and divinity" that was "visible" or "obvious" in creation (1:18-22). They foolishly "exchanged" God's true glory for gods of their own making, idols (1:23, 25; cf. 1:28a). In an initial manifestation of wrath, God "gave over" humans to the overpowering desires of their unfit minds (1:24, 26, 28b; N76). From among the sinful behaviors that increased (1:28-31) Paul singled out a particularly self-evident, appalling, and ironic "exchange" on the horizontal level that paralleled the vertical exchange of God for idols (N77):

> [24]Therefore, God gave them over, in the desires of their hearts, to a sexual uncleanness consisting of their bodies being dishonored among themselves [25]—the very ones who exchanged the truth about God for the lie and worshiped and served the creation rather than the Creator, who is blessed forever, amen. [26]Because of this God gave them over to dishonorable passions, for even their females exchanged the natural use (of the male as regards sexual intercourse) for that which is contrary to nature; [27]and likewise also the males, having left behind the natural use of the female (as regards sexual intercourse), were inflamed with their yearning for one another, males with males committing indecency and in return receiving in themselves the payback (i.e., enslavement to self-dishonoring conduct)

which was necessitated by their straying (from the truth about God to idolatry). (1:24-27; N78)

For Paul, God's wrath was not exhausted in the semipassive act of God stepping back and allowing humans to be mastered by self-degrading passions. By heaping up sins, humans also incur the judgment of "death" that God will inflict on the world at the "day of wrath" (1:32; 2:3-9; 3:5-6; N79). Furthermore, although Paul laid a trap in chapter 2 for the Jewish interlocutor who was judging and yet doing "the same things," Paul did not do so to trivialize sin or put an end to moral judgment. He laid the trap to convict Jew and Gentile of their need for Jesus so that they might receive the Spirit of Christ and be morally transformed (6:1—8:17). God's judgment was still coming on those who practiced the behaviors described in 1:18-32. If God's wrath meant handing humans over to the control of unclean passions, God's salvation must be nothing less than liberation from such passions for a Spirit-empowered life (6:19; N80).

Five arguments can be adduced for ascertaining that Paul in Rom 1:24-27 implicated every form of same-sex intercourse.

1. Intertextual echoes to Gen 1:26-27. Romans 1:18-32 alludes to the creation stories (Gagnon 2001a, 289–93). Romans 1:20 and 1:25 explicitly mention "the creation of the world" and "the Creator," respectively. Romans 1:23 transparently echoes Gen 1:26 (LXX):

> Let us make a human according to our *image* and . . . *likeness;* and let them rule over the . . . *birds* . . . and the *cattle* . . . and the *reptiles.* (Gen 1:26, italics added)

> And they exchanged the glory of the immortal God for the *likeness* of the *image* of a mortal *human* and of *birds* and of *four-footed animals* and of *reptiles.* (Rom 1:23; italics added, N81)

In such a context Rom 1:26-27 surely echoes Gen 1:27 (LXX):

> And God made the human; according to the image of God he made him; *male* (*arsēn*) and *female* (*thēlu*) he made them. (Gen 1:27, italics added)

> Even their *females* (*thēleiai*) exchanged the natural use for that which is contrary to nature; [27]and likewise also the *males* (*arsenes*), having left behind the natural use of the female (*thēleias*), were inflamed with their yearning for one another, males with males (*arsenes en arsesin*). . . . (Rom 1:26-27, italics added)

What is the point of these echoes? Idolatry and same-sex intercourse together constitute an assault on the work of the Creator in nature. Instead of recognizing their creation in God's image and dominion over animals, humans worshiped statues in the image of humans and animals. Similarly, instead of acknowledging that God made them "male and female," some humans went so far as to deny the transparent sexual complementarity of males and females by engaging in sex with the same sex. Those who had suppressed the truth about God visible in creation went on to suppress the truth about themselves visible in nature (N82).

If Gen 1:26-31 is the subtext, then the three main arguments for discounting Rom 1:24-27 are beside the point. With respect to the exploitation and orientation arguments: No homoerotic union could have met with Paul's approval because Paul was looking more at Genesis 1 than at exploitative models in his culture or at a presumption of bisexuality. The main concern for Paul was what same-sex intercourse was *not*—the complementary male-female union ordained by God at creation and revealed in Scripture. A homoerotic union "done well" or with congenital post-fall impulses at work does not satisfy that concern. As regards the misogyny argument, Gen 1:26-31 stresses gender differentiation—essential maleness and femaleness—not gender stratification (N83).

2. *The argument from nature.* Alongside of echoes to Gen 1:26-27, which Paul could expect the Roman believers to pick up (N84), Paul employed an argument from nature to which even "pagans" could be held accountable (Gagnon 2001a, 246–70). Romans 1:26-27 refers to opposite-sex intercourse as "the natural use" of the gendered body and same-sex intercourse as use "contrary to nature" (*para phusin*). What does Paul mean by this? The parallel example of idolatry in Rom 1:19-20 highlights the fact that

> the knowable aspect of God is *visible* (or: obvious; *phaneron*) to them because God *made it visible* (*ephanerōsen*) to them. For from (the time of) the creation of the world, his *invisible qualities* (*ta aorata*) . . . *are clearly seen* (*kathoratai*), *being mentally apprehended* (*nooumena*) by means of the things made.

In other words, visual and mental perception of the material world should lead to certain conclusions about how best to worship God (N85). The sin of idolatry is coupled with the sin of same-sex intercourse because Paul considered both alike to be absurd denials of natural revelation (N86). Together they constitute exhibit A (vertical dimension) and exhibit B (horizontal dimension), respectively, of conscious Gentile suppression of the truth about the Creator's will accessible in the clear, often visible, structures of material creation. In essence Paul is arguing in Rom 1:26-27 that if one did not have access to Genesis or Leviticus one could still recognize in nature that God designed the male-female union alone to be a complementary sexual fit (N87). The evidence from nature—male-female compatibility in anatomy, physiology (e.g., procreative potential), and various interpersonal traits—provides convincing clues regarding God's will for sexual expression (N88).

Once again, the three main pro-homosex arguments for neutralizing Rom 1:24-27 miss the point. A loving disposition and innate attraction are as irrelevant to Paul's critique as they would be to a critique of incest, bestiality, pedophilia, and threesomes. The absence of a gender complement in homoerotic unions constitutes the basis for the indictment. Simply put, male-female intercourse is natural; same-sex intercourse is unnatural to the point of being morally unclean, degrading, and indecent. The only conceivable exceptions for Paul would be instances of same-sex intercourse not involving sex between males or between females—an oxymoron (N89). Moreover, the mere fact that a given desire is innate and resistant to change does not qualify it as "natural" in the sense intended by Paul. The ancients recognized the existence of defects in nature (Gagnon 2001a, 384–85); how much more a Judeo-Christian worldview like Paul's that gave prominence to an anthropological fall from grace. By "contrary to nature" Paul meant anything that did not accord with the divinely intended, well-working processes of nature—including such intractable and congenital sinful impulses as covetousness, envy, and arrogance (Rom 1:29-30). Most people today would understand sociobiologically related urges to have sex with children, close blood relations, or animals as "contrary to nature" in the sense that such unions are structurally incompatible with embodied existence. With respect to the misogyny argument, it is reductionistic to limit Paul's understanding of natural gender complementarity to gender hierarchy, as if sex for Paul were only about who is in control (N90).

3. *The mention of lesbian intercourse.* The fact that Romans 1:26 indicts female-female sex undermines the supposition that Paul was concerned only with certain exploitative forms (N91). Lesbian intercourse in antiquity normally did not conform to the male pederastic model or entail cultic associations or prostitution (Brooten 1996, 361; N92).

4. *Coercion not at issue.* In Rom 1:27 Paul speaks of the mutual gratification of the participants: "the males were inflamed with their yearning for *one another, males with males* . . ." (N93). He also declares that the judgment of God on both partners is

deserved: "males with males committing indecency and in return *receiving in themselves* the payback which was necessitated by *their* straying." Paul was casting his net over every kind of consensual homoerotic activity.

5. *The conception of caring homoerotic unions in Paul's cultural environment.* Every kind of homosexual union imaginable existed in Paul's day. We find glowing tributes to male-male love in the Greco-Roman world, with adult male same-sex unions existing alongside man-"boy" unions (postpubescent; cf. Gagnon 2001a, 350–60; N94). It was well within the conceptual framework of Paul's time to distinguish between exploitative homosexual relations and caring ones. Another problem for those pushing the exploitation argument is that Greco-Roman moralists generally regarded pederastic relationships as *less* exploitative than adult homosexual unions. The "softness" of male adolescence made the violation of the stamp of masculine gender—gender deviance—less pronounced for receptive partners (N95).

These five points demonstrate that Rom 1:24-27 indicts all forms of same-sex intercourse and transcends matters of exploitation, orientation, and misogyny.

First Corinthians 6:9:
Does It Forbid All Forms of Male-Male Intercourse?

First Corinthians 6:9-11 reads:

> Or do you not realize that unrighteous people will not inherit God's kingdom? Stop deceiving yourselves. Neither the sexually immoral (the *pornoi*), nor idolaters, nor adulterers, nor soft men (*malakoi*, i.e., effeminate males who play the sexual role of females), nor men who lie with males (*arsenokoitai*) . . . will inherit the kingdom of God. And these things some of you used to be. But you washed yourselves off, you were made holy (or sanctified), you were made righteous (or justified) in the name of the Lord Jesus Christ and in the Spirit of our God.

Three lines of argument converge to show that 1 Cor 6:9 prohibits all male-male intercourse: word usage, the context of 1 Corinthians 5–7, and inferences from 1 Tim 1:10.

1. *The meaning of* malakoi *and* arsenokoitai. In 1 Cor 6:9-10 Paul expands the vice list in 5:11 by naming three additional groups of sex offenders that fill out the meaning of *pornoi* ("the sexually immoral") beyond participants in incest (ch. 5) and solicitors of prostitutes (6:12-20). The first is *moichoi* (adulterers) and the second and third are *malakoi* and *arsenokoitai*. Five points establish that Paul used *malakoi*, literally "soft men," in the sense of "effeminate males who play the sexual role of females" (Gagnon 2001a, 306–12).

a. Its placement in the midst of other terms that refer to participants in illicit sexual *intercourse*.

b. Its position in the vice list immediately before the term *arsenokoitai*, which clearly refers to the active *homosexual* partner.

c. The severe penalty imposed for being a *malakos* (exclusion from the kingdom of God), which suggests a form of effeminacy well beyond the stereotypical limp wrist (contra Martin 1996, 124–29).

d. The use of cognates by Philo of Alexandria to describe men who actively feminize themselves for the purpose of attracting other men (N96).

e. The use of the comparable Latin term *molles* ("soft men") in tandem with other terms that refer to effeminate males desirous of penetration by men: the *cinaedi* (Gk. *kinaidoi*, lit., "butt shakers") and *pathici* ("those who undergo [penetration]"; see N97). These designations were not confined to adolescents or cult prostitutes, much less did they imply coercion. In fact, they applied especially to *adult* males who *willingly—whether by innate orientation or not*—went to great efforts to feminize their bodies, dress, and manner in order to attract men and thus eradicate the masculine stamp given by nature (N98).

In short, Paul was thinking of the male described in Lev 18:22 and 20:13 who is lain with as though a woman. This background, plus Paul's choice of the term "soft men," indicates that one of the troubling aspects of male-male intercourse for Paul was that it blurred God-given, nature-imbedded gender differences (N99). Issues of exploitation and orientation were beside the point.

As noted earlier (page 67), *arsenokoitai* was concocted from two Greek words in the Septuagint translation of Lev 18:22 and 20:13: "lying" (*koitē*) and "male" (*arsēn*; N100). Only Jews and Christians used the term (N101). A deliberate echo to the Levitical proscriptions is confirmed by 1 Tim 1:10 (below). Consequently, the term "men lying with males" must be every bit as inclusive as these proscriptions (N102). In keeping with the fact that Lev 18:22 addresses the active or penetrating partner, the pairing of *arsenokoitai* with *malakoi* in 1 Cor 6:9 suggests that *arsenokoitai* refers to the active homosexual partner, at least primarily (N103). Ancient Christian literature limits the term to male-male intercourse but, commensurate with the meaning of *malakoi*, not to pederasts or clients of cult prostitutes (N104). This inclusive sense is further confirmed by Rom 1:27, surely the best commentary on what *arsenokoitai* would have meant for Paul. There the contrast is clearly between males who have sex *with females* and males who have sex *with males*—not between exploitative and nonexploitative forms of same-sex or opposite-sex intercourse.

Paul completed the vice list in 6:9-10 with a reminder in 6:11 that the Corinthian believers had been transformed. Some of the Corinthians *used to* engage in incest, solicitation of prostitutes, adultery, and male-male intercourse. Continuance in such practices would endanger their inheritance of the kingdom of God. Such was the case with the incestuous man in 1 Corinthians 5 whose temporary expulsion Paul was now recommending. Issues of "sexual orientation" would have been irrelevant to Paul because the Spirit of Christ was present within to counteract the domination of any sinful impulses operating in the flesh. As Paul stated in 1 Cor 3:1-4, believers are no longer "(mere) humans." They are people of the Spirit—indeed, new creations (2 Cor 5:17). The Spirit does not always eradicate the desires of the flesh—we have not yet shed "the body of sin" (Rom 6:6)—but the Spirit can overcome their controlling influence (Gal 5:16-25). When Paul said "these things some of you used to be" he was not guaranteeing former adulterers that they would never again experience sexual desire for people other than their spouse, or former thieves and swindlers that they would never again be tempted by material possessions. Rather, the point was that they no longer, in the main, lived out of such impulses but rather out of the regulating agency of the Holy Spirit.

2. *The context of 1 Corinthians 5–7* sheds additional light on the inclusive sense of the terms *malakoi* and *arsenokoitai:*

a. **The incest connection in 1 Corinthians 5.** It is likely that Paul intended the vice list in 6:9-10 as a continuation of ch. 5 (the case of the incestuous man) rather than of 6:1-8 (lawsuits before pagans; N105). Paul's strong response to the incestuous man provides an interesting backdrop. I proposed earlier (see p. 48–50) that the Bible's opposition to incest represents the closest analogue to its opposition to same-sex intercourse. Opposition to both converges in the story of Ham, the Levitical sex proscriptions, and some early Jewish texts (e.g., *Letter of Aristeas* 152). Scripture proscribes both sex offenses strongly, and it does so for a similar reason: they involve sex between persons who are structurally too much alike, whether in terms of family or sex. Especially given Paul's allusions to Leviticus 18 in 1 Corinthians 5–6 (see p. 67; N55), it is likely that Paul would have viewed incest as wrong because it was sex with "the flesh of one's own flesh" (Lev 18:6) and realized its structural similarity to male-male intercourse (N106). Just as Paul would not have accepted any kind of incestuous union—loving or not, adult or not, innately predisposed or not—so too he would not have accepted any kind of male-male union. First Corinthians 5 also makes clear how seriously Paul would have taken a homoerotic union within his churches. It would have been grounds for temporary expulsion as a last-ditch measure to bring about repentance and so save the offender's spirit for the kingdom of God (cf. 5:5, 9-11 with 6:9-10).

b. 1 Cor 6:12-20 and the Gen 2:24 connection. Paul cites Gen 2:24b (1 Cor 6:16b) in the immediate context of the probably hypothetical example of a Christian man soliciting prostitutes (6:12-20). The partial quotation "the two shall become one flesh" has in view the entire verse: "For this reason a *man* . . . shall be joined to his *woman/wife*." Just as Paul's indictment of same-sex intercourse in Rom 1:26-27 echoes Gen 1:27 ("male and female he created them"), so too the reference to *malakoi* and *arsenokoitai* in 1 Cor 6:9 is treated in close quarters with the other key creation text (N107). As with Jesus in Mark 10:7-8, so too with Paul: Gen 1:27 and 2:24 are credited with being the defining, prescriptive norms for human sexual expression. Paul obviously understood that Gen 2:24 precluded all types of same-sex intercourse regardless of motive, since intercourse between males attempts to reunite what according to Gen 2:21-23 was never split apart in the first place. First Corinthians 6:12-20 underscores two additional points: (1) Sexual immorality matters because sex always engages the body holistically, even when it involves the relatively impersonal act of sex for money (6:18). One's only recourse is to "flee" it (6:18; cf. Gen 39:12). Sex is not like food; it is never a matter of indifference (6:12-14). (2) The example given in 6:12-20 presumes that a Christian, a person possessed by the Spirit of Christ, can engage in sexual immorality *(porneia)*, whether solicitation of prostitutes, incest, adultery, or same-sex intercourse. Idolatry is not a necessary prerequisite. Nor does being indwelt by the Spirit of Christ automatically validate one's sexual orientation and behavior. On the contrary, Paul equates participation in sexual immorality by a Spirit-possessed believer with having immoral sex in the Holy of Holies (6:15, 19-20); involving the Spirit in immorality intensifies the offense. Hence Paul's insistence in 6:9-10 that believers "stop deceiving [themselves]" into thinking that they can commit gross immorality, repeatedly and unrepentantly, and still inherit God's kingdom.

c. **The marriage connection in 1 Corinthians 7.** In 1 Corinthians 7 Paul discusses only male-female sexual unions because these alone are valid. Sex is to be confined to male-female marriage. Paul made no attempt to regulate positive forms of same-sex intercourse because, quite simply, there were none. Given Paul's liberating approach to wives "having authority over" their husband's body (7:3-4), attempts to attribute his stance against same-sex intercourse to misogyny ring hollow (N108). Moreover, Paul in 1 Cor 7 does not pinpoint procreation as the main reason for sex in marriage. Rather, he views sex in marriage as a healthy outlet for sexual desire that, in turn, relieved some of the internal pressure to commit *porneia* (7:2-7; cf. N109). Consequently, Paul's opposition to same-sex intercourse was not based primarily on its nonprocreative character. At the same time, it would be a logical fallacy to argue, "because of the temptation to immorality, homosexual marriages should be recognized by the church" (Gudorf 2000, 140; N110). Had the Corinthians contended that it was better to allow the adult incestuous relationship of 1 Corinthians 5 to continue than to risk the man's passions boiling over into sexual immorality, Paul would have noted the plain contradiction in terms. An appeal to an incestuous relationship or a homosexual relationship as a means to averting *porneia* is invalid because incest and same-sex intercourse were among the most extreme instances of *porneia*. Neither was wrong in the first instance because of a high potential for promiscuity or infidelity. Each was wrong because it brought together two unnatural, non-complementary sames.

    3. *The contribution of 1 Tim 1:10.* The occurrence of *arseno-koitai* in 1 Tim 1:10 confirms that the term has in view Lev 18:22 and 20:13 since "the law" referred to in 1:9-10 can only refer to the law of Moses (Gagnon 2001a, 334–36). Since the Levitical proscriptions were absolute, the author of 1 Tim 1:10 (whether Paul or a later Paulinist) must have taken *arsenokoitai* absolutely. Scroggs has argued that the preceding term *pornoi* should be given the restrictive translation of "male prostitutes" and the following term *andrapodistai* ("men-stealers, slave dealers, kidnappers") the meaning men who sell boys or girls into slavery at brothel houses. *Arsenokoitai* would then refer only to men who have sex with male prostitutes. However, there is little support for this argument. The last half of the vice list in 1 Tim 1:9-10, at least, corresponds to the order of the Decalogue:

> Fifth commandment (honor one's parents) =
>   "killers of fathers and mothers"
> Sixth commandment (do not kill) = "murderers"
> Seventh commandment (do not commit adultery) =
>   *pornoi, arsenokoitai*
> Eighth commandment (do not steal) = *andrapodistai* (men-stealers)
> Ninth commandment (do not bear false witness) = "liars, perjurers"

    Parallel early Jewish and Christian vice lists and commentaries on the Decalogue establish that *pornoi* refers to "sexually immoral persons" generally and *arsenokoitai* belongs with it under the rubric of the seventh commandment against adultery, while *andrapodistai* finds its place under the distinct heading of the eighth commandment against stealing (Pseudo-Phocylides 3-8; Philo, *Special Laws* 3.1-82; 4.13-19; *Didache* 2:2-3; *Barnabas* 19:4). Accordingly, *arsenokoitai* should be understood in the broadest sense possible. Male-male intercourse is wrong not merely because it tends toward exploitation but because it contravenes the one valid union for sexual expression: a man-woman union.

In conclusion, the combination of *malakoi* and *arsenokoitai* is correctly appropriated for our contemporary context when applied to every conceivable type of male-male intercourse. A similar universal indictment of female-female intercourse is implied (N111). Matters of commitment and orientation, or alleged fears of female authority, were extraneous to Paul's main reason for listing *malakoi* and *arsenokoitai* among those who would not inherit God's kingdom. Same-sex intercourse dishonors God's creation of complementary gendered beings by attempting to reconstitute a binary sexual whole from a single-sex union.

CONCLUDING THOUGHTS

The following major points have been made in this essay:

• Contemporary attempts to impose the acceptance of homosexual practice on the mainline churches will have a devastating multilayered effect.

• Scripture's opposition to same-sex intercourse satisfies the criteria for defining core values, a fact that elevates the burden-of-proof bar considerably high for pro-homosex advocates in the church.

• The analogies commonly used to debunk Scripture's stance on same-sex intercourse—Gentile inclusion, slavery, women in ministry, and divorce/remarriage—are significantly inferior to the analogy of Scripture's opposition to incest.

• Jesus' and Paul's views on love and grace reinforce, rather than reject, the need for strong commandments against sexual immorality, including same-sex intercourse.

• The Old Testament witness against homosexual practice is not only pervasive, absolute, and strong—in marked contrast to the porous views prevailing in the ancient Near East—it is also a largely interconnected and coherent witness.

• Genesis 1 and 2 beautifully image the "one fleshness" of marriage as a *re*union of an original binary sexual whole. Reconstitution obviously requires the joining of the two constituent parts, male and female, which were the products of the splitting.

• Examination of the Sodom narrative in its historical context—fanning out in concentric circles from the text to other material from the same author, then texts in early Israelite literature, then the ancient Near Eastern context, and finally the subsequent history of interpretation—makes clear that the story is not just about gang rape of visitors but also about dishonoring gender integrity. It is about "lying with a man as though lying with a woman" (Lev 18:22; 20:13), treating another's embodied masculine identity as if it were an embodied feminine identity, as if God's differentiation of the sexes in creation amounted to nothing.

• Attempts at dismissing the Levitical proscriptions as prerational and nonethical—belonging to the domain of uncleanness *rather than* sin simply on the grounds of being *categorical* prohibitions—seriously misunderstand how purity taboos operate and lead to ethical absurdities.

• Evidence for Jesus' view can be found in the univocal stances of the Hebrew Bible, early Judaism, and early Christianity; Jesus' position toward the Mosaic law in general and his intensification of sexual ethics in particular; and sayings of Jesus that implicitly proscribe same-sex intercourse. This evidence overwhelmingly supports the conclusion that Jesus' "silence" regarding same-sex intercourse is comparable to his "silence" about incest and bestiality. That is, it is attributable to complete agreement with the sole position found in the Old Testament and early Judaism.

• So far as extant evidence indicates, Paul's stance against same-sex intercourse was not an anomaly within early Christian circles. Rather, it was the view shared by all New Testament writers.

• In Rom 1:24-27 and 1 Cor 6:9 (cf. 1 Tim 1:10), Paul indicted all forms of same-sex intercourse as violations of the prescriptive male-female norm set down in the Genesis creation accounts, in addition to the proscriptions in Lev 18:22 and 20:13.

• Paul argued too, in Rom 1:24-27, that even Gentiles who did not have access to Scripture had no excuse for engaging in same-sex intercourse. For the discomplementarity of female-female and male-male unions—anatomically, physiologically, and inter-personally—was transparent in nature. This provided a much better clue to God's will for human sexuality than the existence of exclusive innate passions.

• That Paul lists, alongside "men who lie with males" in 1 Cor 6:9, "soft men"—adult males who actively feminized themselves in a desire to be penetrated by other men—confirms that a particularly problematic aspect of same-sex intercourse was that it dishonored the embodied stamp of sexual differentiation given by God at creation.

• None of the main arguments used to gut the Pauline witness—exploitation, orientation, or misogyny—addresses adequately Paul's primary reason for opposing same-sex intercourse.

It is one of the great ironies of the modern pro-homosex lobby that it often argues for the insignificance of sexual differentiation while insisting that most homosexuals have a rigid "orientation" toward persons of the same sex. If men and women are really not all that different—I have dialogued with pro-homosex scholars who have made such claims—why is there little attraction to the opposite sex on the part of many homosexuals? For example, in the case of male homosexuality, there must be something distinctively and significantly male in males, a masculine dimension utterly lacking in females, that causes some males to be attracted exclusively to other males and not, for example, to a female who exhibits stereotypically masculine traits. This brings us to the point: persons who are attracted to others of the same sex are erotically attracted to what they intrinsically are as sexual beings. That is morally problematic, just as having sex with one's own mother or sister is morally problematic, regardless of loving intentions.

There is a world of difference between erotic attraction to the sex that one belongs to and erotic attraction to the sex that one does not. *So far as the erotic dimension is concerned* (N112), the former is sexual self-absorption and narcissism or, perhaps worse, sexual self-deception: a desire either for oneself or for what one wishes to be but in fact already is. It is a misguided attempt at completing the sexual self with a sexual same when true integration, as the story of Gen 2:21-24 illustrates, requires a complementary sexual other. "One-fleshness" is not just about intimacy. It is also about structural congruity. A person bearing the stamp of masculine essence is not completed sexually by joining with another who shares that essence. The same is true of two females. Similarly, there is structural incongruity in a sexual relationship between parents and their adult offspring, two siblings, humans and animals, and adults and children.

It is essential to love those who experience homoerotic impulses. Love involves seeking and finding, humbly and patiently coming alongside, remembering one's own failings, having empathy, readily forgiving repeat offenders who repent repeatedly, and putting another's best interests over one's own. However, love does not mean affirming homoerotic acts. Love does not condone any form of behavior that violates Scripture's core values, distorts the structural integrity of the participants, multiplies the risk of serious negative side effects, increases the incidence of the behavior in others through cultural incentives, subjects to persecution those who do not support such behavior, and puts persons at risk of not inheriting God's kingdom.

Nor should the church deceive itself into thinking that it must diminish the aversion to homosexual behavior to make it easier for church members to love homosexuals. Jesus strongly opposed prostitution, adultery, divorce, and, undoubtedly, incest and bestiality. Yet, he did not detest sexual sinners. As with oppressive tax collectors, he tried to reclaim them for God's kingdom. We today continue to have a visceral aversion to incest, even adult consensual incest. This is as it should be. Yet we should not hate those who engage in it. Some argue that it is too hard to be strongly opposed to a given behavior and still love those who commit it. However, doing both is precisely what the gospel is all about. It is the work of Jesus in the world. If the church cannot fulfill that mandate, it should pack its bags. It ceases to be the church, the sphere of Christ's lordship, in any meaningful sense.

It is hard, when one sees another struggling with temptations, not to alleviate the struggle by permitting what Scripture deems sinful. This is especially true in the case of consensual sexual behavior. Yet the worst thing one can do in such circumstances is to try to rescue others from the work that God is doing in their lives. Far from telling us that the life of discipleship would be easy, Jesus stated emphatically that we all have to lose our lives, take up our crosses, and deny ourselves. Paul talked at length about dying to self and recognizing that God's grace is sufficient in our moments of great weakness. The secret of the kingdom of God is that Christ is formed in us most effectively in times of deprivation. We must do what we can to alleviate suffering caused by unfulfilled desire, but always short of violating God's commands. For true life is measured not by getting what we want but by acquiescing to the indwelling Spirit. God has something higher and better in store for us than the satisfaction of fleshly sexual impulses. God is the great Plastic Surgeon; only God is not interested in mere cosmetic surgery but deep-tissue surgery. God wants to change us into the image of Christ by any means necessary. That may mean not always getting what we want, when we want it, and with whom we want it. It will mean nothing less than Jesus.

RESPONSE

to Robert A. J. Gagnon

DAN O. VIA

I appreciate the opportunity for dialogue with Professor Gagnon on this important subject. My first—comparatively long—response will deal broadly with hermeneutical issues, after which I will move to a much briefer treatment of more specific points.

1. HERMENEUTICAL PRESUPPOSITIONS. Professor Gagnon and I are in substantial agreement that the biblical texts that deal specifically with homosexual practice condemn it unconditionally. However, on the question of what the church might or should make of this we diverge sharply. This reveals in a striking way that differences of opinion about the contemporary significance of biblical material strongly depend on the hermeneutical or interpretive principles that interpreters bring *to* the interpretation of Scripture. There is no interpretation apart from the differing presuppositions and starting points from which interpretation is made. No one has Scripture as it is "in itself" but only from a point of view. Therefore, while Professor Gagnon puts great stress on *the* consistent *position* of *Scripture*, his *own position* is a *reading* of Scripture in light of certain ideas and choices that he brings *to* the Bible.

I agree altogether with Professor Gagnon's belief that Jesus and Paul inseparably joined radical grace and forgiveness to the demand for radical obedience and to the judgment against sin that is intrinsic in the latter. I argue, however, that homosexual practice among homosexually oriented, committed couples should not be regarded as sin. Professor Gagnon strongly disagrees because of his unwavering commitment to two intertwined presuppositions that he brings *to* the Bible but that are not required by biblical theology. These two presuppositions are as follows:

Contextual factors. There are *no* contextual factors that can override or disqualify a rule—against homosexual practice—that has already condemned a certain behavior as immoral.

This belief would cause him to discount my use of Scripture to override this rule. Professor Gagnon's accumulative cataloging of the Bible's *pre*scriptive heterosexual norms and *pro*scriptive homosexual norms manifests his commitment to the presupposition under discussion here. But his accumulation of biblical texts condemning homosexual practice is irrelevant to my argument since I agree that Scripture gives no explicit approval to same-sex intercourse. I maintain, however, that the absolute prohibition can be overridden regardless of how many times it is stated, for there are good reasons to override it. And the Jesus of John's Gospel does promise future insights into the gospel that have not been given in Scripture. Perhaps the primary difference between Professor Gagnon and me is our disagreement about what it would take to override a rule in the Bible stated as absolute, about what constitutes weighty evidence—or whether there can be weighty evidence.

Closely related to Professor Gagnon's prioritizing of rules is his decision to focus on homosexual behavior rather than orientation, which decision skews his argument from the outset. All meaning is context-bound, and that is as true for the meaning of acts, decisions, events and experiences as it is for the meaning of texts. When he abstracts homosexual acts from a person's orientation, unifying center of consciousness, or "leading edge"—as John Macquarrie aptly puts it—then he has severed homosexual practice from the most intimate and essential context available and necessary for assessing the quality of the behavior.

I, of course, have also made hermeneutical presuppositions, among them being that there are three factors that, in concert, are powerful enough to override and disqualify the Bible's absolute condemnation of same-sex intercourse: (a) the biblical understanding of creation and redemption and of the bodily-sexual definition of human existence along with the Bible's belief that acts must be understood and evaluated in the light of character; (b) the reality of a destiny created by homosexual orientation; (c) the experience of gay Christians.

Anatomical complementarity. The second of Professor Gagnon's presuppositions that I want to address is his frequently employed argument that same-sex intercourse violates nature in the sense that it subverts the divinely intended complementarity and fittedness of penis and vagina that God has made manifest in the material creation. This theme is neither as prominent nor as graphically articulated in this article as it is in his book, but it is still present, and it comes from his preunderstanding, not from the biblical texts.

The Bible does not describe the male and female sexual organs and certainly does not speak of their fit. Nor does Rom 1:24-27 even hint that intercourse contrary to nature is a violation of the anatomical complementarity. That is Professor Gagnon's *interpretation,* and it *may* be part of what Paul had in mind and would seem to be in some significant part correct for us—but not wholly correct, and it is not in the text. Professor Gagnon attributes it to the biblical texts because that is what he *believes* the texts *must* mean, but the belief and the meaning come from his own modern set of beliefs.

The fit of male and female sexual organs is clearly self-evident for us. I have shown, however, that in the New Testament there are dimensions of human life that are too complex, subtle, puzzling, unexpected, and ironic to be accounted for solely on the basis of what is self-evidently obvious. If we turn our *imaginations* toward this complex mystery, we can think of morally justifiable sexual connections that lie outside the palpably manifest anatomical complementarity of penis and vagina. Professor Gagnon does not imagine this possibility. We should recall Amos Wilder's reminder of several decades ago: "The road to moral judgment is by way of the imagination."

I have fully acknowledged that the Gospel of John does not literally or directly support my argument to justify homosexual practice among committed couples. But the canonization of the biblical books assembled them into a kind of single text. Within this multiplex configuration the various parts impinge upon each other so that the Johannine categories provide weighty theological material that can override the biblical rejection of all homosexual practice.

I believe that there is a logical semantic connection between "abundant life" and "all truth," on the one hand, and my defense of committed homosexual practice, on the other. That is, abundant life is such an all-embracing idea that it can include the specific actualization of whatever bodily-sexual orientation one has been given by creation, and similarly all the truth revealed in Jesus is sufficiently all-encompassing to include an understanding of sexuality that could not have been grasped in the biblical setting. (1) Responsible homosexual practice and (2) the ethical justification of it are specific instances, respectively, of the broader categories (1) abundant life and (2) all the truth, instances that do not put undue semantic strain on the historical meaning of the Johannine concepts.

2. AFFLICTION. Professor Gagnon's reference to those "afflicted" with homoerotic desires suggests—regrettably—that homosexual orientation is a disease.

3. CHANGE. Despite what he may affirm about the reality of homosexual orientation, he nevertheless seems to regard homosexual passions as mutable.

4. ANALOGIES. Whatever may be the merits of Professor Gagnon's critique of analogies—Gentile inclusion in the church, slavery, women in ministry, and so on—used by other members of the "pro-homosex lobby" to support the legitimacy of responsible homosexual practice, his critique does not affect my position, for I make no use of those analogies.

5. PURITY AND SIN. Professor Gagnon emphasizes the similarity and compatibility between uncleanness or impurity and sin and holds that Paul properly maintained the concept of impurity in his moral discourse and did not reinterpret impurity as sin. I pointed in my paper to a significant overlapping between uncleanness and sin, but they also diverge sharply on a crucially important point that Professor Gagnon pays virtually no attention to. Uncleanness happens automatically from contact with a physical object or process without any subjective involvement or intention on the part of the person. Sin, on the other hand, proceeds from the conscious will and understanding of the heart.

In Rom 1:18-28 the *uncleanness* to which the wrath of God gives people up proceeds from the *heart* and entails the conscious, intentional suppression of truth and rejection of God. Moreover, this uncleanness is parallel to and inclusive of such *moral* faults as covetousness, malice, envy, murder, deceit, heartlessness, etc. Clearly Paul does reinterpret uncleanness as sin by attributing the nature of sin to the word "uncleanness." Professor Gagnon tacitly acknowledges this, despite himself, in that he distinguishes ritual impurity, which he believes Paul rejects, from moral impurity, which he believes Paul maintains. It seems impossible to distinguish moral impurity from sin in its moral manifestation.

6. HEARING THE GOSPEL. A proclamation of the gospel that is oriented to Professor Gagnon's interpretation of "Homosexuality and the Bible" will be heard differently by heterosexuals and homosexuals. Heterosexuals will hear: God extends to you forgiveness and the restoration of fellowship and empowers you to actualize *all* of the possibilities for good offered in your created destiny. You are liberated to enact your sexual identity. But remember that God requires that you realize all these possibilities for good in a morally responsible way.

Homosexuals will hear: God extends to you forgiveness and the restoration of fellowship and empowers you to actualize *all* of the possibilities for good offered in your created destiny. There are, however, no possibilities for good in the enactment of *your* sexual destiny. God requires you to realize your possibilities for good in a morally responsible way, but there is no morally responsible way for you to realize your sexual identity. Thus you are "liberated" *from* the actualization of your sexual destiny. Or to put it in a slightly different way: Since you had the bad luck to turn out gay, it is only fair to impose the added burden of denying you the realization of who you are sexually.

I would hope for a proclamation of the gospel in relation to human sexuality that can be heard in the same way by homosexuals and heterosexuals: God extends to you forgiveness and restoration and empowers you to realize all the possibilities for good given in your created destiny. Remember that you are required to actualize these possibilities in a morally responsible way. You are liberated *for* the enactment of your sexual identity and—it is hoped—*from* forces in church and society that would compel you to deny who you are.

RESPONSE

to Dan O. Via

ROBERT A. J. GAGNON

I welcome the opportunity to interact with Professor Dan Via (N113). I have five main areas of concern.

USE OF THE BIBLE

Professor Via calls the Bible "the highest authority for Christians in theological and ethical matters," but then establishes his own sense of what is "existentially engaging and compelling" as the highest authority. Via never develops a method for determining what matters in Scripture that is capable of constraining his subjectivity (N114). He appears indifferent to whether an ethical position is held marginally in Scripture or is maintained pervasively, strongly, absolutely, and counterculturally (N115).

Via severely underestimates the extent and degree of Scripture's opposition to same-sex intercourse. He ignores the interconnectedness of an array of anti-homosex Old Testament texts (Gagnon 2001a, 54-110). He contradicts himself on the Sodom and Gibeah narratives—claiming both that they are only about "homosexual gang rape" and that they show a strong aversion to *any* male's serving as the passive partner in male-male intercourse. Via ignores the clear implications of Gen 1:27 and 2:21-24 for an opposite-sex prerequisite, as well as their prescriptive reuse by Jesus and Paul (N116). He ignores the multiple pieces of evidence for what Jesus and New Testament writers other than Paul thought about same-sex intercourse (N117), not to mention the witness of early Judaism (Gagnon 2001a, 159-83). Despite insisting on the importance of literary and historical contexts, his claim that one need override only a "few explicit biblical texts" indicates a considerable disregard for context concerns.

PURITY, SIN, AND ABSOLUTE RULES

The Levitical Holiness Code does not categorize male-male intercourse "as a source of uncleanness *rather than* as sin." It categorizes *sin* in chapters 18 and 20 as moral impurity (N118).

Via acknowledges that Paul operates from an ethical viewpoint. Yet Paul no more takes into account *loving* disposition than do the Levitical prohibitions (cf. 1 Corinthians 5; N119).

Leviticus 18:22 and 20:13 prohibit male-male intercourse because it makes another male a man's sexual counterpart ("the lyings of a woman"; N120). Paul similarly rejects same-sex intercourse because it violates the Creator's intention (Genesis 1–2) and suppresses the truth about male-female complementarity transparent in nature (N121). Sex is not just more intimacy. It is about re-merging with one's sexual "other half" into a sexual whole—as Gen 2:21-24 teaches. The logic of sexual intercourse requires two complementary sexual halves (N122).

Given Paul's absolute, "structuralist" stance (N123), it is absurd for Via to allege that Hays, Jones and Yarhouse, and I have moved homosexual practice "out of the range of sin," "where Paul [had] correctly put it," and "into the range of uncleanness" (N124).

Neither Mark 7:14-23 nor Rom 14:14 elevates a loving disposition over absolute sex prohibitions. Food entering a person's stomach does not defile but a violation of God's sexual requirements does (N125).

Via rejects "absolute rules"—rules that make no exceptions for loving intent. Logically, then, Via should consider on a case-by-case basis all sexual relationships between a man and his mother (or full sister). Nor could he hold the line on monogamy (N126).

Via is an absolutist about no absolutes (N127). He insists that the church must be able to override *all* rules in one or more contexts. *Nothing* is "intrinsically immoral." Such thinking, if carried to its logical conclusion, would lead to dangerous corollaries that I suspect not even Via would accept, such as maintaining that not even rape, sex with one's parent or a prepubescent child or an animal, or racism are intrinsically immoral (N128).

Via alludes to a misogynistic quality in the biblical prohibition of same-sex intercourse. However, that gender differentiation and not gender stratification was the main concern is evident from the creation stories and from a comparison of Paul's views on women with those on same-sex intercourse (N129). Ultimately, the misogyny argument leads to the illogical corollary that Jews and Christians were the biggest misogynists of their day (N130).

THE BIBLE AND HOMOSEXUAL ORIENTATION

According to Via, Paul regarded "homosexuality as chosen," knew about only a heterosexual "nature or orientation," and viewed same-sex intercourse as contrary to this "nature."

Nothing in the language of Rom 1:24-27 suggests that "homosexuality" is a *chosen* condition of constitutional heterosexuals (N131). The *exchange* and *leaving behind* (1:26-27) refer *not* to a choice of homosexual *desire* over heterosexual desire but to a choice of *behavior* stimulated by disoriented passions over behavior motivated by nature. *Nature* in this context is male-female complementarity clearly revealed in the material creation (N132). Collectively, the language of *exchanged, leaving behind, God gave them over, desire,* and *inflamed with their yearning* suggests passions that are pre-existing, controlling, and exclusive (N133).

There were many theories in the Greco-Roman world posit-ing biological influence on the development of one or more forms of homoerotic behavior—Platonic, Aristotelian, Hippo-cratic, or astrological (Gagnon 2003, VI, A.; N134). Causation factors included a creation splitting of male-male or female-female binary humans, a particular mix of male and female "sperm" elements at conception, a chronic disease of the mind or soul influenced indirectly by biological factors and made hard to resist by socialization, an inherited disease analogous to a mutated gene, sperm ducts leading to the anus, and the particu-lar alignment of heavenly constellations at birth.

Differences with contemporary theories (N135) have no bear-ing on the overall point: Many in the ancient world believed that some homoerotic practice could be traced to interplay between biology and nurture; moreover, that homoerotic impulses could be very resistant to change (N136). Paul was probably aware—as was Philo—of the existence of a lifelong homoerotic proclivity given his reference to the *malakoi* (adult "soft" men; N137). The burden of proof is on Via to establish otherwise (N138).

Via claims that, if Paul knew about something akin to homo-sexual orientation, he was logically inconsistent in labeling same-sex intercourse "contrary to nature." This is false (N139).

First, even some of the Greco-Roman texts theorizing biolog-ical influence designated the activity as contrary to nature (N140). Not everything given *by nature* is constituted *according to nature*; persons' desires can be at odds with their essential sex (N141). Second, *nature* for Paul meant something structurally broader than "sexual orientation" (N142). Third, even exagger-ated claims about homosexual orientation are compatible with Paul's view of sin in Romans 5 and 7 as an innate impulse, oper-ating in the human body, transmitted by an ancestor human, and never entirely within human control. For Paul these elements did not disqualify an impulse from being sinful; they rather defined sin as sin (N143).

THE BIBLE AND SCIENCE

Via complains that Jones and Yarhouse and I deny to science "any significant part in deciding about ethical issues." This is not only inaccurate (N144) but also ironic since Via does much less with, and seems less informed about, the scientific literature (N145).

Scientific evidence indicates *at most* an indirect and secondary congenital influence on homosexual development (Gagnon 2001a, 396-413; N146). Certainly no one is born a homosexual, though Via talks as if homosexual desire were an inevitable part of God's creative intent in nature (N147).

In children exhibiting significant gender nonconformity (N148), early proactive intervention can decrease the chance of homosexual development (Gagnon 2001a, 408-13; N149).

Sociological studies suggest that the incidence of homosexuality varies widely depending on the degree of societal support or rejection of homosexual activity (Gagnon 2001a, 413-18). Via has not addressed this.

The vast majority of self-identified homosexuals will experience some heterosexual attraction at some point in life (Gagnon 2001a, 418-20); so much for a general presumption of fixity (N150).

Therapeutic success in treating the homoerotically inclined may be no less than for a number of other relatively entrenched conditions such as alcoholism or pedophilia (Gagnon 2001a, 420-29; N151). Therapists define *success* as management of unwanted desires, not complete elimination. *Change* is multifaceted (N152).

Among consenting adult sexual behaviors that the church discourages, homosexual behavior has perhaps the worst track record for increased risks of demonstrable harm. Few consensual behaviors *always* produce scientifically measurable, significant, and lasting harm. It is enough to establish disproportionately high rates (Gagnon 2001a, 452-60, 471-83; N153).

Without being cavalier, the gospel assures all believers that God can convert sinful passions of the flesh *from* debilitating hindrances *to* redemptive, Christ-forming moments of eternal worth (N154).

THE ALLEGED BIBLICAL CASE FOR HOMOSEXUAL PRACTICE

Via alleges that Gagnon "does not grant to the opposing biblical material the same authority that he grants to the rule against same-sex intercourse." The problem here is that there is no "opposing biblical material" (N155).

1. "Human existence is essentially bodily," yes, but we are not to live "according to the flesh" (Rom 8:12-14). Many ingrained bodily impulses are part of the flesh to be crucified in Christ (N156).

2. *Sexuality* is *a* defining feature of human existence but *gratifying* sexual desires is not (N157). Ironically, Via tries to make his case in (1) and (2) from Scripture texts that operate only on the assumption of, and indeed promote, an absolute heterosexual prerequisite: Gen 1:27; 2:24; and 1 Corinthians 6–7 (N158). Scripture should be understood contextually on this point.

3. The alleged "immutability" of homoerotic desires does not justify equating homosexuality and heterosexuality in "God's creative intent" (N159). *Destiny* for Christians is determined by *God's* purposes at creation and for re-creation, not by whatever seemingly intractable urges humans might have. *Reorientation* is the order of the day (see N160 for seven other points).

4. In Johannine thought life is not just something Jesus gives. It is something that Jesus is (N161). The Gospel of John critiques the idolatrous belief that persons need something (sex, status, etc.) besides Jesus in order to experience abundant life (Gagnon 2001b, 2–3; N162). Again, the text of the Gospel of John should be read contextually (N163).

The New Testament's references to the unexpected do not constitute "a critical challenge" to *Paul's* appeal to the self-evident complementarity of male and female (which includes, *but is not limited to*, the sex organs; N164). There is a big difference between God working in unexpected ways and God working in ways diametrically opposed to Scripture's core values (N165).

The case for an absolute proscription of homosexual behavior is made in the same way that one makes the case against incest: Scripture + nature (structural congruity arguments) + disproportionately high problems = a case for total proscription (N166).

5. The burden of proof has not shifted to those who side with the overwhelming testimony of Scripture. Let Via and Martin *prove* that withholding approval of same-sex intercourse does more damage to persons than providing cultural incentives for homosexual activity. The evidence to date suggests otherwise (Gagnon 2001a, 452–60, 471–89; N167).

6. What Via is advocating is not a mere "reinterpretation of tradition" but outright refutation of a—perhaps *the*—chief pillar of biblical sex ethics; namely, that God intended sexual intercourse to be for the remerging of two sexual halves into "one flesh." Via's refutation is not the Holy Spirit leading us into all truth. It is the spirit of the world leading us back into slavery to "immutable" passions of the flesh—in short, a return to Egypt.

Humans are not robots or mere animals. Their choices are not limited to enslaving impulses of the flesh. God's moral will cannot be held hostage to human sexual libidos. Jesus—not any alleged constitutional predisposition—is Lord.

Select Bibliography

Barr, James. 1973. *The Bible in the Modern World*. New York: Harper & Row.

Barrett, C. K. 1968. *A Commentary on the First Epistle to the Corinthians*. Harper's New Testament Commentaries. New York: Harper & Row.

Bellis, Alice Ogden, and Terry L. Hufford. 2002. *Science, Scripture, and Homosexuality*. Cleveland: Pilgrim.

Bird, Phyllis A. 1997. "The End of the Male Cult Prostitute." In *Congress Volume: Cambridge 1995*. Edited by J. A. Emerton, 37–80. Supplements to Vetus Testamentum 66. Leiden: Brill.

———. 2000. "The Bible in Christian Ethical Deliberation concerning Homosexuality: Old Testament Contributions." In *Homosexuality, Science, and the "Plain Sense" of Scripture*, ed. David Balch, 142–76. Grand Rapids: Eerdmans.

Boswell, John. 1980. *Christianity, Social Tolerance, and Homosexuality*. Chicago: Univ. of Chicago Press.

Brooten, Bernadette J. 1996. *Love between Women: Early Christian Responses to Female Homoeroticism*. Chicago Series on Sexuality, History, and Society. Chicago: Univ. of Chicago Press.

Bultmann, Rudolf. 1955. *Theology of the New Testament*. Vol. 2. Trans. Kendrick Grobel. New York: Scribners.

Conzelmann, Hans. 1975. *1 Corinthians*. Trans. James Leitch. Hermeneia. Philadelphia: Fortress Press.

Countryman, L. William. 1988. *Dirt, Greed, and Sex: Sexual Ethics in the New Testament*. Philadelphia: Fortress Press.

De Young, James B. 2000. *Homosexuality: Contemporary Claims Examined in Light of the Bible*. Grand Rapids: Kregel.

Dodd, C. H. 1953. *The Interpretation of the Fourth Gospel*. Cambridge: Cambridge Univ. Press.

Dodds, E. R. 1968. *The Greeks and the Irrational*. Berkeley: Univ. of California Press.

Douglas, Mary. 1979. *Purity and Danger: An Analysis of Concepts of Pollution and Taboo*. London: Routledge.

Edwards, George R. 1984. *Gay/Lesbian Liberation: A Biblical Perspective*. New York: Pilgrim.

Fredrickson, David E. 2000. "Natural and Unnatural Use in Romans 1:24-27: Paul and the Philosophic Critique of Eros." In *Homosexuality, Science, and the "Plain Sense" of Scripture*, edited by David Balch, 197–241. Grand Rapids: Eerdmans.

Fretheim, Terence E. 2001. "The Old Testament and Homosexuality: What Is God Doing?" In *The Lutheran* (May): 54–55. A fuller 8,000-word version is available online at http://www.thelutheran.org/0105/page55.html.

Furnish, Victor P. 1979. *The Moral Teaching of Paul: Texts and Hermeneutics*. Nashville: Abingdon.

———. 1994. "The Bible and Homosexuality: Reading the Texts in Context." In *Homosexuality in the Church: Both Sides of the Debate*, edited by J. Siker, 18–35. Louisville: Westminster John Knox.

Gagnon, Robert A. J. 2000. "A Comprehensive and Critical Review Essay of *Homosexuality, Science, and the 'Plain Sense' of Scripture*, Part 1." *Horizons in Biblical Theology* 22: 174–243. [Part 2 forthcoming in the Dec. 2003 issue.]

———. 2001a. *The Bible and Homosexual Practice: Texts and Hermeneutics*. Nashville: Abingdon.

———. 2001b. "The Bible and Homosexual Practice: Theology, Analogies, and Genes." *Theology Matters* 7.6 (Nov/Dec): 1–13. Online: http://www.theologymatters.com/TMIssues/ NovDec01.PDF.

———. 2002a. "Are There Universally Valid Sex Precepts? A Critique of Walter Wink's Views on the Bible and Homosexuality." *Horizons in Biblical Theology* 24:72–125.

———. 2002b. "Gays and the Bible: A Response to Walter Wink." *Christian Century* 119.17 (Aug. 14–27): 40–43. Fuller version and rejoinder online: www.robgagnon.net.

———. 2003. "Does the Bible Regard Same-Sex Intercourse as Intrinsically Sinful?" In *Christian Sexuality,* edited by R. E. Salzman, 106ᴺ55. Minneapolis: Kirk House.

Greenberg, David F. 1988. *The Construction of Homosexuality.* Chicago: Univ. of Chicago Press.

Greene-McCreight, Kathryn. 2000. "The Logic of the Interpretation of Scripture and the Church's Debate over Sexual Ethics." In *Homosexuality, Science, and the "Plain Sense" of Scripture,* ed. David Balch, 242–60. Grand Rapids: Eerdmans.

Gudorf, Christine E. 2000. "The Bible and Science on Sexuality." In *Homosexuality, Science, and the "Plain Sense" of Scripture,* ed. David Balch, 121–41. Grand Rapids: Eerdmans.

Hays, Richard B. 1986. "Relations Natural and Unnatural: A Response to John Boswell's Exegesis of Romans 1." *Journal of Religious Ethics* 14:184–215.

———. 1996. *The Moral Vision of the New Testament: Community, Cross, New Creation, a Contemporary Introduction to New Testament Ethics.* San Francisco: HarperSanFrancisco.

———. 1997. *First Corinthians.* Interpretation. Louisville: John Knox.

Jewett, Robert. 2000. "The Social Context and Implications of Homoerotic References in Romans 1:24-27." In *Homosexuality, Science, and the "Plain Sense" of Scripture,* edited by David Balch, 223–41. Grand Rapids: Eerdmans.

Jones, Stanton L., and Mark A. Yarhouse. 2000a. "The Use, Misuse, and Abuse of Science in the Ecclesiastical Homosexuality Debates." In *Homosexuality, Science, and the "Plain Sense" of Scripture,* ed. David Balch, 73–120. Grand Rapids: Eerdmans.

———. 2000b. *Homosexuality: The Use of Scientific Research in the Church's Moral Debate.* Downers Grove: InterVarsity.

Koester, Craig R. 1993. "The Bible and Sexual Boundaries." *Lutheran Quarterly* 7:375–90.

Macquarrie, John. 1986. "Destiny." In *The Westminster Dictionary of Christian Ethics,* ed. James F. Childress and John Macquarrie. Philadelphia: Westminster.

Malherbe, Abraham J. 1986. *Moral Exhortation: A Greco-Roman Sourcebook.* Library of Early Christianity 4. Philadelphia: Westminster.

Martin, Dale B. 1996. "*Arsenokoitēs* and *Malakos:* Meanings and Consequences." In *Biblical Ethics and Homosexuality: Listening to Scripture,* ed. Robert Brawley, 117–36. Louisville: Westminster John Knox.

Mauser, Ulrich W. 1996. "Creation and Human Sexuality in the New Testament." In *Biblical Ethics and Homosexuality: Listening to Scripture,* ed. Robert Brawley, 3–15. Louisville: Westminster John Knox.

Melcher, Sarah J. 1996. "The Holiness Code and Human Sexuality." In *Biblical Ethics and Homosexuality,* ed. Robert Brawley, 87–102. Louisville: Westminster John Knox.

Milgrom, Jacob. 2000. *Leviticus 17–22.* Anchor Bible 3A. New York: Doubleday.

Moore, Stephen D. 2001. "Sex and the Single Apostle." In *God's Beauty Parlor and Other Queer Spaces in and around the Bible,* 133–72. Stanford: Stanford Univ. Press.

Neusner, Jacob. 1973. *The Idea of Purity in Ancient Judaism.* Studies in Judaism in Late Antiquity 1. Leiden: Brill.

Nissinen, Martti. 1998. *Homoeroticism in the Biblical World: A Historical Perspective.* Minneapolis: Fortress Press.

Nolland, John. 2000. "Romans 1:26-27 and the Homosexuality Debate." *Horizons in Biblical Theology* 22:32–57.

Outka, Gene. 1972. *Agape: An Ethical Analysis*. Yale Publications in Religion 17. New Haven: Yale Univ. Press.

Powell, Mark Allan. 2003. "The Bible and Homosexuality." In *Faithful Conversation: Christian Perspectives on Homosexuality*, edited by J. M. Childs, 19–40. Minneapolis: Fortress Press.

Ricoeur, Paul. 1967. *The Symbolism of Evil*. Trans. Emerson Buchanan. Boston: Beacon.

Schmidt, Thomas E. 1995. *Straight and Narrow? Compassion and Clarity in the Homosexuality Debate*. Downers Grove: InterVarsity.

Schoedel, William R. 2000. "Same-Sex Eros: Paul and the Greco-Roman Tradition." In *Homosexuality, Science, and the "Plain Sense" of Scripture*, ed. David Balch, 43–72. Grand Rapids: Eerdmans.

Scroggs, Robin. 1983. *The New Testament and Homosexuality: Contextual Background for Contemporary Debate*. Philadelphia: Fortress Press.

Smith, Mark D. 1996. "Ancient Bisexuality and the Interpretation of Romans 1:26-27." *Journal of the American Academy of Religion* 64:223–56. [Responses by Daniel Helminiak and James E. Miller, with Smith's rejoinder in *JAAR* 65 [1997]: 855–70.]

Soler, Jean. 1979. "The Dietary Prohibitions of the Hebrews." *New York Review of Books* 36/10 (14 June).

Swartley, Willard M. 2003. *Homosexuality: Biblical Interpretation and Moral Discernment*. Scottdale, Pa.: Herald Press.

Tillich, Paul. 1951. *Systematic Theology*. Vol. 1. Chicago: Univ. of Chicago Press.

Toulouse, Mark G. 2000. "Muddling Through: The Church and Sexuality/Homosexuality." In *Homosexuality, Science, and the "Plain Sense" of Scripture*, ed. David Balch, 6–42. Grand Rapids: Eerdmans.

Trible, Phyllis. 1978. *God and the Rhetoric of Sexuality*. Overtures to Biblical Theology. Philadelphia: Fortress Press.

Via, Dan O. 1990. *Self-Deception and Wholeness in Paul and Matthew*. Minneapolis: Fortress Press.

Waetjen, Herman C. 1996. "Same-Sex Relations in Antiquity and Sexuality and Sexual Identity in Contemporary American Society." In *Biblical Ethics and Homosexuality*, ed. Robert Brawley, 103–16. Louisville: Westminster John Knox.

Walsh, Jerome T. 2001. "Leviticus 18:22 and 20:13: Who Is Doing What to Whom?" *Journal of Biblical Literature* 120:201–9.

Webb, William J. 2001. *Slaves, Women, and Homosexuals: Exploring the Hermeneutics of Cultural Analysis*. Downers Grove. InterVarsity.

Williams, Craig A. 1999. *Roman Homosexuality: Ideologies of Masculinity in Classical Antiquity*. New York: Oxford Univ. Press.

Wink, Walter. 1999. "Homosexuality and the Bible." In *Homosexuality and Christian Faith: Questions of Conscience for the Churches*, edited by Walter Wink, 33–49. Minneapolis: Fortress Press.

———. 2002a. "To Hell With Gays?" A Review of *The Bible and Homosexual Practice* by Robert A. J. Gagnon. *Christian Century* 119.13 (June 5–12):32–34. Online: www.robgagnon.net.

———. 2002b. "A Reply By Walter Wink." *Christian Century* 119.17 (Aug. 14–27):43–44. Online: www.robgagnon.net.

Wold, Donald J. 1998. *Out of Order: Homosexuality in the Bible and the Ancient Near East*. Grand Rapids: Baker.

Wright, David F. 1984. "Homosexuals or Prostitutes? The Meaning of [*Arsenokoitai*] (1 Cor. 6:9, 1 Tim. 1:10)." *Vigiliae Christianae* 38:125–53.

Index of Scripture

OLD TESTAMENT

GENESIS

1–3	61–62
1–2	72, 100
1	61, 89
1:26-31	78
1:26-27	31, 32, 62, 77, 79
1:26	77
1:27	71, 78, 85, 100, 104
2–3	46
2	89
2:7	30
2:18-24	61, 65
2:20	61
2:21-24	91, 100
2:21-23	85
2:24	31, 32, 61, 71, 85–86, 104
2:24b	85
3:1-7	5
3:14-19	11
9:20-27	57
19:1-29	5
19:1-9	56
19:4-11	60
39:12	85

EXODUS

14:12	29
22:21	45
23:9	45

LEVITICUS

11:9-12	7
11:13	8
12:1-5	7
12:4	6
15:1-12	7
15:16-30	7
15:18	7
15:19	6, 7
17–26	6, 51
17–18	75
17:1	9
18	57, 58, 63, 64, 66, 72, 84, 100
18:1	9
18:3	8
18:6-18	7
18:6	48, 85
18:12	75
18:19	66
18:20	66
18:22	5, 7, 8, 11, 13, 56, 62, 63, 67, 83, 87, 89, 90, 100

18:23-30	66
18:23	7
18:24-30	64, 66
18:24	8
18:25	66
18:26	63
18:27	8
19:1	9
19:2	11
19:11-12	10
19:17	10, 51
19:18	50, 51, 63, 70
19:19	7
20	64, 72, 100
20:1	9
20:10-16	64
20:13	5, 7, 11, 13, 56, 62, 63, 67, 83, 87, 89, 90, 100
20:17	57
20:25	8
22	66
25:39	45
25:42	45
25:55	45
36	66

NUMBERS

13:20—14:4	29
14:8-13	29
14:15-16	29
14:19	29
14:22-23	29
14:33	29
29:22	6

DEUTERONOMY

6:5	50
15:15	45
22:5	60
23:17-18	59, 73
23:18	60

JUDGES

19	5
19:13	6
19:22-25	56, 60

1 KINGS

4:32-33	17
14:21-24	59
15:12-14	59
22:46	59

2 KINGS

23:7	59

JOB

36:13-14	59

PSALMS

19:1-2	17

PROVERBS

6:16-17	11

ECCLESIASTES

1:2	23
3:11	23
4:1-4	23
8:17	23
11:5	23

ISAIAH

1:2-5	5
1:4	5
1:5-9	11

JEREMIAH

5:23	5
7:9-10	11
7:13-14	5

JEREMIAH (*continued*)

13:10	5
17:1	5
17:9-10	5

EZEKIEL

16:47-52	11
16:49-50	57
16:50	58
17–26	58
18	58
18:7-8	11
18:10-13	58
18:12	58
18:22	58
18:24-30	58
22:11	58
33:26	58

AMOS

4:1	6
5:11-12	6
6:4-6	6

APOCRYPHA

SIRACH

| 38:1-8 | 17 |

WISDOM

| 7:15-22 | 17 |

NEW TESTAMENT

MATTHEW

5:17-20	52
5:17-18	69
5:27-32	51
5:27-28	71
5:29-30	53, 71
5:32	47, 71
6:4	35
6:6	35
6:18	35
7:6	73
7:12	70
7:15	35
7:17-18	20
8:5-13	68
10:14-15	73
10:38	52
10:39	52
12:33-35	20
12:39-41	73
13:29	35
18:21-22	52, 70
19:9	47
22:38	51
23:23	69
23:26	20

MARK

1:44	69
3:34-35	52
7	9
7:14-23	100
7:15-19	69
7:18-23	20
7:21-23	72
8:21-22	52
8:34-37	52
9:43-48	20, 53, 71
10:1-12	71
10:6-9	32

10:6-8	31, 71
10:6	62
10:7	61
10:11-12	71
10:17-22	72
12:10-11	35
12:30-31	50

LUKE

6:31	70
7:1-10	68
7:36-50	70
10:10-12	73
10:28-35	70
11:29-32	73
11:42	69
14:27	52
16:16-17	52
16:17	69
16:18	71
17:3-4	52, 70
17:33	52

JOHN

1:2-3	35
1:3	34
1:11	34–35
3:16	34
3:36	34
4	70
5:24	34
6:47	34
6:54	34
7:53—8:11	70
10:10	34
11:25-26	34
12:25	52
14:26	39
15:26	39
16:12-13	39
17:3	34

ACTS

10:34-35	17
15	44
15:20	75
15:29	75
21:25	75

ROMANS

1–11	53
1	22
1:18—3:20	76
1:18-32	13, 77
1:18-28	9, 97
1:18-22	76
1:18	13
1:19-32	76
1:19-20	13, 17, 79
1:20	77
1:21-27	11
1:21-23	24
1:21-22	13
1:21	13
1:21b	13
1:23-27	62
1:23	76, 77
1:24-27	13, 24, 25, 55, 67, 74, 76-81, 89, 90, 95, 101
1:24	13, 14, 76
1:25-27	14
1:25	13, 76, 77
1:26-27	14, 32, 78, 79, 85, 101
1:26	13, 76, 80
1:27	80, 83
1:28-32	24
1:28a	76
1:28b	13, 76
1:29-30	80
1:32	77
2:1—3:20	76
2:3-9	77
2:5-6	13
2:14-15	17
3:5-6	77

ROMANS (*continued*)

5	102
5:12-21	26
5:12	24
6:1—8:17	53, 77
6:1-14	53, 54
6:6	84
6:15	53, 54
6:16-23	53, 55
6:19-23	53
6:19	54, 55, 77
6:20-23	55
7	102
7:4-6	54
7:5-6	53, 55
7:5	24
7:7-23	26
7:9-24	24
8:1-17	53, 54
8:1-7	26
8:2	54
8:12-14	54, 55, 104
8:16	30
12:1	56
14:14	67, 100
15:1-2	36

1 CORINTHIANS

1:26-29	35
2:10-11	30
3:1-4	84
5–7	55, 56, 67, 82, 84-87
5–6	84
5	68, 75, 83, 84, 85, 86, 100
5:5	85
5:9-11	85
5:11	82
6–7	104
6:1-8	84
6:9-11	55, 81
6:9-10	11, 12, 13, 82, 83, 84, 85, 86
6:9	67, 74, 81–88, 89, 90
6:11	83
6:12-20	53, 82, 85–86
6:12-14	85
6:13	30
6:15	30, 86
6:16	61
6:16b	85
6:17	30
6:18-20	56
6:18	22, 24, 85
6:19-20	86
6:20	45
7	86–87
7:1-2	31
7:2-7	86
7:2	17
7:3-4	86
7:3	31
7:5	31
7:7-8	31
7:9	17
7:10-11	71
7:10-16	47
7:19	56
7:21-23	45
7:23	45
7:28b	31
7:32-33	31
8:9-13	24
9:21	54
10:24	36
10:33	36
11:14	22
12:4	36
12:8-11	36
12:31	36
13:1-13	36
13:1-7	36
13:3	35
13:5	36
16:18	30

2 CORINTHIANS

2:13	30
5:15-21	54
5:17	84
7:13	30
8:8-12	36
12:21	55

GALATIANS

2:19-20	54
2:20	53
3:28	46
5:13-26	53
5:16-25	84
5:18	54
5:19-21	55
5:22	36
5:24-25	54
6:2	54
6:7-9	55

EPHESIANS

4:17-19	55
5:3-6	55

PHILIPPIANS

2:4	36
3:10-11	54
3:20	54

COLOSSIANS

3:5-10	55

1 THESSALONIANS

4:1-8	44
4:2-8	55
4:3-8	67
5:15	36

1 TIMOTHY

1:9-11	55
1:9-10	87
1:10	12, 74, 82, 83, 87–88, 89, 90

PHILEMON

16	45

2 PETER

	75
2:7	59
2:10	59

JUDE

	75
7–8	59
7	58, 59
8	58

REVELATION

	75
21:8	59
22:15	59, 73